KEEPERS OF
THE POOR

J. Edward Carothers

contents

FOREWORD 5

INTRODUCTION 13

CHAPTER I. "THE FUTURE POURING IN" 15
    What Is the Future? 16
    The Kingdom of God 18
    "War Against Poverty" 21
    Christian Concern 24

CHAPTER II. THE POOR WHO ARE IN POVERTY 26
    The Poor Are Outcasts 27
    The Poor Are Indecent 29
    The Poor Are Hostile 30
    Conversion Needed 33
    The Poor Are Unlovely 34

CHAPTER III. WHY DO PEOPLE STAY POOR? 36
    "Poverty-linked Characteristics" 38
    Unchristian Attitude 40
    Poverty in Rural Sections 43

CHAPTER IV. WHY RELIEF AND WELFARE FAIL 47
    New Ministry 49
    Personal vs. Community Ideals 52
    Shift in Work 55

CHAPTER V. HOW CAN POVERTY BE BANISHED? 58
    The *Road* 59
    Office of Economic Opportunity 63
    Resources of the Church 65

CHAPTER VI. THE CONVERSION OF THE PROSPEROUS. 68
    Guilt from Prosperity 69
    Goal of Psychiatry 70
    Church Members and Guilt 73
    Transformation of "Self" 76

CHAPTER VII. THE CHURCH IN ITS CONVERTING
    ROLE 78
    What Is a Disciple? 80
    Two Steps for the Church 83
    Church Renewal Demand 86

CHAPTER VIII. THE INDIVIDUAL CHRISTIAN AND
    SOCIAL STAGNATION 90
    Characteristics of Society 92
    Duties of Individual Christians 96
    Congregational Duties 98
    Duties of Institutions 101

CHAPTER IX. THE POOR WHO CROWD THE GLOBE . 105
    Poverty-Population Law 107
    A Third Proposition 109
    Global Hunger 111
    Political Position 114
    The Nature of the Church 117

CHAPTER X. WHAT THE METHODISTS ARE DOING .. 119
    Methodists and Education 122
    Community Centers 123
    Residences 125
    Hospitals 126
    Appalachia 127
    Protestant Slowness 130
    Missionaries in Action 131
    Methodist Committee for Overseas Relief 133

CHAPTER XI. WHAT THE METHODIST CHURCH
    SHOULD BE DOING IN THE WAR ON POVERTY .. 135
    The Local Church 136
    The Methodist Denomination 141
    The Interdenominational Level 148

THEOLOGICAL POSTSCRIPT 151

FRIENDSHIP PRESS MATERIALS 153

BIBLIOGRAPHY 155

INDEX 159

TO

Bruce

Terrie Lee

Jonathan

Jennifer Lee

Karen Lee

and to Sarah Parrott, a fine editor

foreword

It was a lucky day when the talented cartoonist and social critic, Jules Feiffer, created the sequence which constitutes the opening pages of this book.* In the cartoon the prosperous man confesses his manifold sins and wickedness to the poor man, and in Feiffer's final drawing manages to make himself feel that he has really become involved.

Social criticism can be a game, with everyone playing a part and with no one being truly involved in real life. This book is an attempt to open up to all of us our private and social condition. The first nine chapters may hurt us in spots.

But we need to face our opportunities. No generation before us has had our chance to eliminate poverty from the national scene and make a start on its riddance on the world level. A thousand years from now historians will rank this period as one of the truly great times in man's struggle to make this world a place fit for God's children to walk in.

We have the bomb to cope with but we also have nuclear power to make fresh water out of the sea, produce fertilizer out of the air and turn the wheels of industry from pole to pole.

It is our great chance. We must take it. No longer will it do any good to beat our breasts and wail about our failures. By now we know how bad we have been. It is now time to find out how good humanity can become in the exercise of plain, ordinary common sense and with the Son of Man to lead us in the responses we now make to the kingdom of God that is literally pouring in upon all mankind.

---

* Cartoon by Jules Feiffer used by permission of the Hall Syndicate, Inc., 30 E. 42nd St., New York, N.Y. 10017.

LOOK, MISTER, I ASK YOU NICE FOR A QUARTER TO CALL MY KIDS OUT OF TOWN.
IS MY WAY OF LIFE SO MORALLY SU-PERIOR THAT I CAN PREACH TO YOU ABOUT THE BREAKDOWN OF YOUR FAMILY? I HARDLY KNOW WHO MY PARENTS ARE AND I LIVE WITH THEM!

introduction

The basic argument of this book is that the attitudes of the prosperous keep the poor in poverty. This is not an argument to produce comfort, but the data supporting it are so heavy that we cannot avoid facing up to it.

It may be that a few prosperous people would like to keep some others poor so as to have cheap labor for yards, kitchens and industries. Prosperous people of this type surely must be in the minority, which means that our keeping people in poverty is not intentional. It means also that the social attitudes of the prosperous people who read this book are acceptable to them, and that they do not realize that these attitudes are such as to keep people in poverty.

Not many poor people will read this book. Later on we will go into a more detailed definition of "poor." It is enough, at this point, to say that not many books are bought and read by members of a family of four living on a yearly income of $3,200.00. On the other hand, many people who "feel" poor may read this book. Some of us have very little spare cash and consequently we often "feel" poor. We have, however, convinced ourselves that we have a definite concern for those even poorer than we. This book will be an irritant to some in this latter group.

Church people in the United States are not ordinarily among the poor. When we remember that 80 per cent of our population is considered prosperous, we are forced to admit that a very high proportion of our church people also are prosperous. This book assumes that almost everyone who studies it or obtains a copy of it is among the prosperous.

Christians would be the first to admit that they should be their brother's keeper. They would also be quick to agree that they should keep the poor out of poverty whenever possible. The title of this book is intentionally used to say that while Christians should keep the poor out of poverty, their prevailing

13

attitudes make them keepers of the poor *in* poverty. This indictment was not intended when this book was first undertaken. It is an argument formed as data were unfolded and examined. In a certain sense, this book took things into its own hands as it was being written and is therefore a product of its data.

It may be that some readers will feel that they are under attack. The writer also has felt himself to be under attack. It is an uncomfortable experience to write a book that increases one's sense of guilt, which has been the experience of the author of this book.

Most of us have been feeling increasingly guilty about poverty in this country and in the world. Numerous studies indicate that in or near 1945 our capacity to produce goods in the United States passed the point where we could technically supply all our people with more than enough to eliminate poverty from every home. Our power to produce is undisputed. Our power to distribute to all our people food, clothing, shelter, education and medical care—as well as other social goods—has not equaled our power to produce these goods.

This book is a diligent effort to ask once more: "What is wrong in our approach to the issue of poverty in our nation and the rest of the world?"

A major limitation of this book is its dominant reference to the United States. The author has read many of the major publications dealing with world poverty, but his orientation is, unfortunately, rather limited. It would seem, however, that in a general way the analysis proposed here applies to the entire world. In order to avoid thinning out the analysis, major reference is made to the United States, but readers who know more about other countries may find that what applies to the attitudes of the prosperous in this country also applies elsewhere.

This book is an effort to put a finger on the problem of poverty in a world that cannot afford to let poverty continue, and it ends with the finger pressing uncomfortably hard upon the center of our prosperous lives.

chapter I

"THE FUTURE POURING IN"

It would be a waste of time to discuss the problems of poverty in purely economic or sociological terms. There are dozens of books that do so. The only justification for a Christian study book on this subject is that the Christian religion has a direct relationship to the problem of poverty.

The distinguishing feature of Christianity is its central Person, Jesus of Nazareth. The distinguishing feature of his ministry was his preaching of the kingdom of God. It is his interpretation of the kingdom of God that constitutes our strategy in the war against poverty.

Unfortunately, Christians in the twentieth century have, almost universally, the wrong idea of what Jesus meant by the kingdom of God. The popular notion that the kingdom of God is something we can build if only we are good enough and work hard enough is, in my opinion, wrong. Jesus never taught that anyone could build the kingdom of God, and he did not invite people to help him try to build it.

We are greatly indebted to many New Testament scholars for their efforts to correct the false notion that Jesus thought that the kingdom of God is a kind of society that can be built, if Christians were only busy enough and intelligent enough to build it. Among the great contemporary scholars who have sought to correct this notion are C. H. Dodd of Cambridge, Joachim Jeremias of Göttingen and W. D. Davies of Union Theological Seminary, New York. Dr. Davies writes:

". . . the message of Jesus had two facets, the declaration that the Kingdom of God had drawn near and the call to radical repentance. And it is here, we suggest, that the secret of the radicalism of Jesus' demand lies. Not any immanent end of the universe, not any principle of creation, not any casuistry,

15

led Jesus to his understanding of God's will. He passed beyond all principles he had inherited, beyond the light of Law and Prophet, to what we can only call an intuitive awareness of the will of God in its nakedness. This awareness he expressed in terms of the immanence or presence of the Kingdom of God." [1]

It is absolutely necessary for us to understand this statement. Professor Davies is saying that the kingdom of God is not something we build, *it is God's will that has already moved in upon us to demand our answer to its conditions.* No wonder Jesus preached a gospel that took as its first word, "Repent." What else can we do when God's will moves in upon us and catches us at whatever we may be doing? There we stand, naked in our enterprises, caught in surprise because the kingdom of God always comes, as Jesus said it did, "as a thief in the night."

Language is important. Finding the right words to get to the heart of an idea is hard for us. It may be helpful to think of the kingdom of God as the future pouring in, baptizing all that exists with both judgment and grace.

What Is the Future?

Let us begin a brief examination of this way of saying that the kingdom of God is "upon us" by asking what we mean by the *future.* Most people think of the future as an empty room that can be furnished according to our power and skill. Others talk about "carving out the future" as if it were a great, untouched block of marble awaiting our masterly craftsmanship.

Any number of thoughtful people have been taking a different view of the future. In *The Future as History* Robert Heilbroner notes that we no longer see history as "the expected culmination of the past, as the growing edge of the present." [2] Heilbroner notes, too, that there is a certain unpredictability about events. The plans of yesterday are thwarted by today's

---

[1] W. D. Davies, *The Setting of the Sermon on the Mount* (Cambridge: Cambridge University Press, 1964), pp. 431-432. Used by permission.
[2] Robert Heilbroner, *The Future as History* (New York: Harper and Brothers, 1959), p. 15. Used by permission.

unexpected intrusions. In a certain sense, today is flooded with the necessity for making decisions we never dreamed we would have to make. In recognition of this element of existence Jesus cried, "Repent, the kingdom of God is at hand." He added, "Believe the good news!" He was saying that a penitent attitude toward the present while it is being baptized by "the future pouring in" is the right attitude if one is to make the best possible decisions for the lines of action requiring one's commitment now.

A major religious problem of our time is the inability of people to understand conditions as the future pours in upon us. Kenneth Boulding unfolds the magnitude of what is now happening in his book, *The Meaning of the Twentieth Century*. Boulding says that we are in the second great transition in the history of mankind.

"The first transition was that from precivilized to civilized society. . . . This is a transition that is still going on in some parts of the world, although it can be regarded as almost complete. Precivilized society can now be found only in small and rapidly diminishing pockets in remote areas. It is doubtful whether more than 5 per cent of the world's population could now be classified as living in a genuinely precivilized society.

"Even as the first great transition is approaching completion, however, a second great transition is on its heels. It may be called the transition from civilized to post-civilized society." [3]

Boulding describes the post-civilized society as one featuring technology. He does not lament the passing of civilization because it has been a hard period for most people. He recognizes the difficulties of having anything better in the post-civilized period, but maintains that there is at least a technology that might be used for the good of mankind.

The point is, no one expected this to happen. Mankind did not decide to gird up his collective loins and walk directly into a "future" such as we now have on our hands. What happened

[3] Kenneth Boulding, *The Meaning of the Twentieth Century* (New York: Harper and Row Publishers, Inc., 1964), pp. 1-2. Used by permission.

was a fruition of mankind's efforts within a cosmic situation that engaged in having its own influences on what now abounds. The future poured in upon mankind—and still does. "Behold, the kingdom of God is among you."

Alvin Toffler, lecturer on mass communications and social analyst, says that one of the basic problems affecting human life right now is the psychological inability to handle the "future," and he calls the ailment "future shock." He notes that people suffering from this ailment cannot deal rationally with environment. He adds, "I believe that malaise, mass neurosis, irrationality, and free-floating violence already apparent in contemporary life are merely foretastes of what may lie ahead unless we come to understand and treat this psychological disease." [4]

The Kingdom of God

The Christian doctrine of the kingdom of God is a means of escaping from "future shock" because it enables a person partly to understand his own times. Jesus was not concerned primarily with mental health. He was concerned mainly with obedience to the will of God. But he understood the will of God in a way that makes the mind healthy. For Jesus, the will of God was found in the conditions of the present situation that required man's response, in penitence and faith (joy).

Harvey Cox follows Amos Wilder in saying, ". . . the coming of the Kingdom presented itself in the form of claims requiring the renunciation of certain things and the acceptance of a new discipline of discipleship." [5] In different language, this is to say that the kingdom of God is found in the unfolding situations of life where God demands our decision. In short, the future pours in upon us, and we have to decide what we will do with the work on our desk, the crops in the field, the smog in the air and the child in the crib. All that we have done up to

---

[4] Alvin Toffler, "Future as a Way of Life," *Horizon,* (Summer 1965) 7:108-115, p. 109. Used by permission.
[5] Harvey Cox, *The Secular City* (New York: The Macmillan Company, 1965), p. 112. Used by permission.

now is defective; nonetheless, we have to make more decisions and do something. If we just sit, stand, gaze, remain aloof, we will perish. Nor can we act in the sure confidence that we will always do the right thing. And so we "repent, and believe the good news" that while judgment hovers over every act, grace likewise abounds, and it may be that what we do will be for blessing and not for curse.

Günther Bornkamm puts it: "God's reign is hidden from us, and must be believed and understood in its hiddenness. Not in any way the apocalypticists thought, beyond the heavens, in the bosom of a mysterious future, *but here, hidden in the everyday world of the present time, where no one is aware of what has already taken place.** Of this Jesus speaks in his parables of the Kingdom of God." [6]

According to Jesus, it is God's will that we act for others whether or not it pays off in cash or personal advancement. Bonhoeffer speaks of Jesus as "the man for others" and makes the point that a true "man for others" will act for "others" even to the point of going beyond where God can be of any help to him. Witness Jesus on the Cross, where his own conduct had taken him, at last to the point where he had to be on his own (without any help at all) to save others. This, truly, is religion "come of age."

In the war against poverty the contemporary Christian is often discouraged by the facts surrounding him. Poverty is as widespread as it was thirty, fifty, sixty years ago. On the world-wide level it is probably going to grow worse before it has been even slightly reduced. Our hopes sometimes are betrayed by corruption and mismanagement in programs designed to reduce poverty. Often we are more easily discouraged by setbacks in the war against poverty than in wars of other kinds. We expect a certain amount of human folly in business, government, education and church life, but in regard to expressions

---

* Dr. Carothers' italics.
[6] Günther Bornkamm, *Jesus of Nazareth* (New York: Harper and Brothers, 1960), p. 69. Used by permission.

of humanitarian good will, such as the war against poverty, the foibles of man are harder to accept.

If we understand that the present conditions of life requiring our decision represent the kingdom of God that has literally poured in upon us as a kind of future flooding the present, then we may be able to understand that the kingdom of God includes some elements not wholly desirable to us. We do not like poverty and we do not like mismanagement, but the kingdom of God is upon us, and we have to make decisions about poverty and mismanagement. We may not like the contrasts between affluence and poverty, but the kingdom of God is come, and we have to respond to the conditions that wait for our decision.

Christian people should not suffer from "future shock" if they understand that the conditions prevailing in any particular moment constitute the kingdom of God. Conditions require decisions in penitence for what is past and in joy for what can be done.

This means that our approach to the problem of poverty in the world is based upon a theology, a doctrine of the kingdom of God, a doctrine of the future pouring in upon us, with its baptism of judgment and its offering of grace. Under this doctrine we cannot desert in the war against poverty nor do we want to do so. We have to find out where we stand under God's judgment in the war and how we stand in relation to God's grace as we seek a victory.

Only a foolish person should fail to see what it means to allow poverty and affluence to exist side by side in the same society. Thousands of potential volcanoes are waiting to erupt in the United States and elsewhere around the world. When the residents of the Watts area of Los Angeles burst into rebellion during August, 1965, they were saying to the rest of us in no uncertain terms that they were no longer willing to live like rats.

It is not enough for us to realize that rebellion is brewing in the world, with the poor being set against the prosperous. There is no great difficulty in arousing people to fear one another. This has been done to gain a real grasp of the issue: the future has poured in upon us, and poverty must be ended, or there will be hell to pay.

Congressional legislation leading up to the adoption of the Economic Opportunity Act, and the creation of the Office of Economic Opportunity, is a long overdue recognition of the dangerous cancer eating at the vitals of our society. Widespread fear of the future made it "good politics" to write and pass the legislation, which was supported by both parties. The value of a law is neither limited nor increased by saying that it was "good politics" to adopt it. "Good politics" may mean that legislation has such wide public support that failure to enact it would mean "bad politics," and no administration will engage deliberately in "bad politics."

War Against Poverty

Something had happened in this country before the anti-poverty legislation was adopted. Almost a decade before the war against poverty was declared, the churches held consultations on what were then called "pockets of poverty." While these meetings produced groundbreaking data about the invisible poor, it was not then known that poverty does not exist in "pockets" but spreads like a blanket, invisible but real, across the land. Publication of the findings of various consultations and foundation inquiries began to produce similar data, and the gradual buildup of national anxiety resulted finally in the Economic Opportunity Act.

The atmosphere which launched the war against poverty was as interesting to observe as it is important to understand. It was by no means exclusively an atmosphere of compassion; it was also an atmosphere darkened by the fear that all these poor people constituted a menace. These were the people who did not consume the products of our factories, and these were the people who committed a high proportion of our crimes. These were the ones who roamed the streets and did not attend school.

In the next chapter we deal more directly with this attitude toward people in poverty. It is enough to say at this point that the poor were generally regarded as a threat to our nation's welfare, and on this basis we set out to do something about it.

This in itself revealed an ill-grounded attitude toward the future because it assumes that prosperous people can manipulate the future in terms of their skills and powers. In other words, the prosperous set out to solve the problem of poverty—the problem thought of as existing in people who are poor and in poverty. It so happens that this is not where the problem is located. The problem is located in the prosperous whose attitudes keep the poor in poverty. Through our failure to understand that the future pours in with judgment upon *all that is,* we isolated the problem in the wrong place. Blame for being poor was put upon the poor, and the prosperous decided that the best that could be done with the poor was to make them prosperous whether they liked it or not.

There is no point in discussing the problem of the prosperous and the poor in our time unless we do it in terms of the future, as it pours in upon us with judgment and grace. It is stark madness to assume that we who are prosperous can bring the poor into line with what *we* think, want, and do.

Should we train young people now in poverty for factory jobs that decline in number every year? Should we train them for professions that may no longer exist in their present form? Do we educate people for working with computers? If so, what computers? The period of gestation for new computers is roughly equal to that for a human life: nine months.

When we understand the nature of our century we see readily that in our generation a miracle in history has occurred. The present hour is not a continuation of the long and dimly traced past. The present moment marks a new departure. The word for the present historical situation is "disjunction." This means that the rails upon which we now begin to ride are not connected directly to the rails upon which we have been riding. Is this true because man is a clever being? Is this brought about by the bright little animal whose yesterday was spent in caves without lights? Is the evolutionary development of man only a push from inside his brain and skin, with an empty void we call the future waiting for the exercise of human skill and power, as man himself determines? Or is the evolutionary development of man enveloped in a reality that will not let him "get by" unless he grows toward an increasingly human existence in life? The future pours in upon man and explodes, ravishes, devours or otherwise exerts itself in judgment upon all his work that is inhuman. Yet it also flows with graciousness to enrich every advance toward a new support of humanity.

Whether man survives, and continues on the planet for a few more million or billion years, will be determined by his response to the future. At this point in human history, issues are emerging that make the hour exciting with prospects for a new kind of social life on the planet. The issues of nuclear war, population increase, prosperity-poverty are not separate from each other but are connected with great vitality. They cannot possibly be understood as social issues or political issues alone. They are issues of motivation and human self-understanding. They are theological issues.

It is encouraging to observe that Christianity is not the only world religion taking new note of the issues of life and death. Some Christians are worried about the renewed vitality of Islam and Buddhism. This vitality may mean problems for Christian expansion, and it is certainly quite clear that Christianity will be a minority faith for a long time to come. This may be necessary in order to save Christianity from becoming too intimately identified with the great, emerging power structures of the planet. Power in our world tends to concentrate in positions of enormous authority. Courageous witness will be required to obtain critical evaluation of dominant power structures. This kind of witness may be possible only if Christianity speaks from a minority position.

Christian Concern

A major distinction of Christianity, as contrasted to other great religions, is its concern for people who suffer pain inflicted by systems. In recent years the World Council of Churches, the Vatican and the various national councils of Christian churches have manifested an increasing awareness that human life must be protected from the cruelty not only of persons but also of systems—political, economic, ecclesiastical, judicial or cultural.

Embodied in this Christian concern is an attitude toward the future which needs to be made a lively philosophy, if we are to escape "future shock." In particular, we need a framework that will enable us to deal with the complex problem of why people stay in poverty. As long as we believe that it is possible for every individual to "carve out his own future" (as we who are prosperous tend to think we have "carved out our own future") we will be blind to what is happening to us and around us.

For a long time we have had dinned into our ears that "no man is an island unto himself" and we are sick of hearing the bell toll for us. But we need to open our hearts and minds to the fact that the human race is not an island unto itself and that the bell is not tolling in the distance. The future is roaring in upon us as never before, flooding the human enterprise. Among the great issues confronting our generation is the one that will have to be settled now between the prosperous and the poor.

For the prosperous to believe that the poor will be manufactured into duplicates of the current prosperity-type is evasion of the truth. The human race refuses to be molded. Furthermore, the poor are more intelligent than to want to duplicate the kind of life the prosperous have "carved out" for themselves.

The pouring in of the future cannot be stopped, wished away, argued away or ignored. The day of the Lord has arrived and, as Amos noted, it is a most unexpected event. It provokes in us the kind of surprise felt by a man who leans against the wall, in a dark room at night, only to be struck by a viper lying in waiting. We are in a world described by the National Council of Churches' Conference on Technology and Rapid Change as a "world that won't hold still." The conference might have described it even more forcefully as "a world God won't leave alone."

The term "keepers of the poor" has two meanings. The prosperous *keep the poor in their poverty,* but they have a definite responsibility *to be their brother's keeper,* and to break his chains of poverty. The poor cannot break their chains because they are forged of the hardened attitudes of the prosperous who seldom, if ever, realize that their attitudes constitute the chain.

The prosperous are in need of a major conversion of attitudes, which begins with a changed attitude toward the future. The Christian view of the future, dealing with realities and offering a base for optimism, is that man's efforts toward any goal are fruitful when values are created and sustained in support of human life. The Christian view holds also that the destruction, or hindrance, of such support is visited by the wrath of the future, for God is the future acting upon the present.

It is hoped that this book will be a test of individual ability to engage in honest self-scrutiny. The test will be painful for all prosperous individuals as they face the collective responsibility imposed upon them by the facts.

We who are keepers of the poor should face up to the charge of "Guilty." This is the only way in which we can be saved from the *wrath* of God, the future pouring in. This is also our only means of receiving the *grace* of God, also the future pouring in. We can choose only between being victims or victors. We cannot make the choice as to the nature of the terms. We must cease being keepers of the poor and become our brother's keeper.

chapter II

THE POOR WHO ARE IN POVERTY

Not so long ago I was told by a man working among some of the poorest people in this country that there is not a chance in the world that prosperous people will ever be able to understand what it means to be poor. My informant even went so far as to say that he personally had not been able to identify with the poor people with whom he lives and to whom he has fully committed his life. I can only guess at what he meant by this, but I think he meant that the person who is not poor is incapable of knowing what poverty is like, and that the person who is poor cannot possibly know what it is like to be prosperous.

It is mainly to this issue that I wish to direct our thinking, but as a preliminary consideration I wish to indicate a line of definition that marks the poor. According to a statement made by R. Sargent Shriver, Jr., Director of the Office of Economic Opportunity, on Monday, May 3, 1965, the poor are to be defined as those in a family of 4 whose combined income is less than $3,130 per year, or a single person whose income is under $1,540 per year. This would put a family of 2 at about $1,990 per year, and a family of 3 at about $2,440 per year.

This standard was set in reply to criticisms from the United States Chamber of Commerce that previous definitions were not satisfactory. For example, it was claimed that a family of 4 in the South may often live comfortably on $3,000 per year if it grows its own food. The Chamber of Commerce had said also that the arbitrary rule of $3,000 set some families in the category of being poverty-stricken, which stigmatized and disheartened them.

However, we must have yardsticks to measure our problems, and taking Mr. Shriver's measurement for a moment we discover that 34.6 million people in this country live in poverty, and that of this number 70 per cent are white persons. It should be added that of this vast number of persons at least 15 million are children.

It is my urgent purpose at the outset of this book to discover whether or not we, the writer and the reader, together can become emotionally alive to a set of social conditions that easily finds us intellectually responsive. Therefore, I will strive to do what my friend told me we cannot do, namely, develop a valid empathy with the poor.

It seems to me that this is necessary, because what we *know intellectually* about poverty must be accompanied by *deep emotional involvement* if we are to wage what appears to be a long and difficult war against it. Another term for emotional involvement might be existential awareness, or we might say that we are dealing with personal identifications of one kind or another. In any case, my motive is to project myself into the life of the poor and, I hope, take my reader with me.

I could begin by saying that in my family we have been poor, *if* we speak of economic factors only. We have gone without food for as long as five days. We have had to build our own shelter on the prairie, and once we went through a blizzard too cold for some to survive, but somehow the rest of us did live with the aid of four lumps of coal and heavy comforters. *Poor* we have been, but not *in poverty*, for we knew even at the time that we belonged to the larger community. We had connections in the world of the prosperous through family, education, cultural experience and the like. In the true sense of the word we were destitute, but we were not poor. We were in need but not in poverty, for to be in poverty is to suffer an actual dislocation from the larger community.

The Poor Are Outcasts

To be poor is, first of all, to be outcast. The poor person in poverty is an outsider and knows it. During a research project some of the individuals in the project dressed as do the poor, and went into the street to ask for direction to other streets. They were literally brushed off by everyone to whom they spoke. When they returned in the garb of the prosperous they received all the information they needed.

The poor do not belong to the larger community in any respect. A few weeks ago I visited a Methodist mission project and talked with a woman in the mountains of Kentucky. She saw her first physician after she had given birth to her eighth child. When told by one of our workers that she was being taken to the doctor, she remarked without much emotion, "It ain't fer me." What she meant was that this was an experience she considered quite appropriate for others, but not for herself, just as most of us do not expect to go to the moon but may readily expect others to do so.

Most of us expect something. Hope is natural to the prosperous disposition. The poor do not expect what we expect, nor do they hope for what we hope. They expect to be poor, uncomfortable, in continual struggle with unmet needs and unpayable debts, if they are able even to owe anything to anybody. They expect hourly what we seldom give thought to in our most anxious hours: the pounding fist of the landlord demanding his rent, the sound of rats in the wall at night, the threat of unmitigated pain. They cannot have such hopes as ours because their world is utterly unlike ours. You and I are kinsmen chiefly in what we hope for. Indeed, we are brought to the writing and reading of this book more by our hopes than by our past experiences, for there is much of the past that we do not hold in common, but we have a shared dream of what may come to pass if we can work together.

The poor dare not hope because to have hope and be unable to realize that hope is to suffer much pain. "Work without hope is like nectar in a sieve" (Indian proverb). The only salvation for the hopeless is to give up working and hoping and accept the barren conditions that deny the hope. This the poor must do to remain sane.

Some people refer to such loss of expectation and hope as lack of motivation. This seems to imply that motivation is a kind of super-fuel put into a person's "tank of life" as a source of energy. To be motivated it is necessary to have expectation and hope. These the poor do not have as do the prosperous because the poor live in a different world, in which they remain generation after generation. "Three generations on welfare" is easy to understand, for all of us tend to live on in the only world we know, and the only world the poor know is the world into which they have been cast—the world of poverty. No wonder it is called "the other America" by some and the "invisible America" by others.

The Poor Are Indecent

The second characteristic of being poor is being considered by the prosperous to be indecent. The prosperous make contact with people in poverty, in the most convincing way, to prove to the poor that they are indecent. When a candidate for high political office attacks the poor on grounds that they are indolent and shiftless, the attack registers. When a newspaper editorial charges that the poor are worthless and should be forced to do something for themselves, this strikes home to an audience not always able to buy copies of the evening edition. News unfailingly reaches its subject. How it does so is something of a mystery, but the poor know what the prosperous think of them.

One of the main purposes of the parables of Jesus (according to Joachim Jeremias, *The Parables of Jesus*, pages 100 ff.) was to defend his preaching against the charge that he had offered the gospel to indecent people, including the poor. The poor were considered lazy, indifferent, unendowed, under-endowed, and so forth. We use such terms today. Not for one moment did the larger community in the time of Jesus consent to the proposition that the poor were in their plight because of the attitudes of the prosperous. *Jesus introduces this note into his preaching!* He said that the rich can hardly enter the kingdom of God, but the poor are among the blessed.

This was radical thinking, and it is even more radical today, because in our world the poor are considered indecent by the prosperous, who fail to realize that the fate of the poor is not entirely their own doing, but is in large degree an accident of birth and circumstance.

The poor finally lose their sense of self-worth and consent to the proposition that they are indecent. The spiritual condition of feeling indecent keeps poor people out of our conventional churches and drives them into the addictions, the social hostilities and the other tragic estates of mind and soul that turn them into statistics about which the prosperous worry.

The Poor Are Hostile

This leads us to a third point. Many years ago I planted a blue spruce in front of my little church in a small western town. It was cut down in the dark hours of the night by a young man whom I was trying to help, and whose family was notoriously poor. The young man also entered the little church, plugged the sink drain and turned on the water, flooding the basement. Why did he do this when I was trying to be helpful? Today I know the answer. He hated me in my prosperity.

A little while before that I had found a Mexican family living in a tin shelter in a Colorado sugar beet field. Two children lying in a heap of rags on the dirt floor were blind from starvation. I worked with them for days to get medical help, food and some kind of shelter from the winter. One night the man stole my car. That was a long time ago, and I began early to understand that the poor cannot help having hostility toward the prosperous, because they have self-directed hostility in enormous force that must be turned against another, or it will lead to the destruction of their own self. Hatred of the prosperous is, in a certain sense, the only alternative to self-hate or suicide for the poor, trapped in their self-rejection.

Self-rejection and consequent hostility toward the larger community of prosperity are not attributes of the poor simply because they lack economic goods. They tend to hate themselves and others because they know they are outcast, considered indecent and unwanted in the larger community. Until these psychological elements that operate in poverty are recognized by the prosperous, no amount of economic aid will suffice to save the poor from their fate in a society of prosperity. Self-directed hostility was markedly operative in the Watts area of Los Angeles during August, 1965, when the poor set fire to scores of buildings in their own part of the city.

It is by no means unusual to hear people say that the poor in their poverty could at least keep clean, obey the law, and take better care of the houses they manage to rent from the prosperous. These they cannot do. It might be a wise assumption that the poor will always be compelled, by unconscious psychological forces, to violate the established values cherished by the prosperous. How else can they express their contempt and hostility? What is left for them, excepting their refusal to submit to the demands of the prosperous? And so they spit in the street, throw their rubbish out the window, break the door off its hinges and feel better because of relieved hostility.

The hostility pent-up in the ranks of the poor in this country is going to be unleashed, and there are at least two reasons for thinking so. The Economic Opportunity Act offers a means whereby the poor become the concentrated concern of prosperous people who say, in effect, that they want the poor to stop being poor. To ask the poor to cease being poor is to ask them to do much more than clamber into the economic bracket and spending habits of the prosperous. One does not move from poverty to prosperity simply through a shifting of the amount of money available for spending. The poor may not know this, nor do the prosperous seem to recognize it. As a consequence, the prosperous are unwittingly urging the poor to change their ways, while contemplating no change in their own ways. The prosperous do not realize that it is largely their attitudes and expectations that condemn the poor to live in poverty. The community of the poor was created to a large extent by the

31

fixed attitudes of the prosperous. As Oscar Ornati has so vividly pointed out, the poor do not have a port of entry into the larger community of the prosperous. Yet, there is now a nation-wide demand that the poor shall resemble the prosperous, without becoming intruders in the community of the prosperous, or at least not until all their habits, cultural patterns and spiritual attitudes are identical with those now prevailing among the prosperous.

This incompatibility of the demands of the prosperous with the inabilities of the poor to change radically in habit and manner points toward a possible unleashing of latent hostility on the part of the poor. It could take almost any form, but in any case it will likely be directed against the social structures and value systems cherished by the prosperous. In both urban and rural situations, the repudiation of conventional values by the poor is already far advanced, and the release of the full force of suppressed hostility is made more likely by the nation-wide demand that the poor change their way of life.

The other indication that we may witness an unleashing of the latent hostilities of the poor is the considerable success of the community organization movement now generally identified with Saul Alinsky. This is not the place for a detailed evaluation of all that is involved, but it should be said that the rather re-markable success of the movement may in a large measure be attributed to the fact that the poor have enough hostility within them to be responsive to being organized. As some would put it, enough is hurting the poor to make them respond to being organized in order to get power. Only a generalized notion of power through community organization is necessary to arouse an hitherto passive community-grouping into a thoroughly energetic organization. What happens in this case cannot be explained merely in terms of the skill of an organizer, although this must be taken into account. What counts most is that the poor are hostile enough to be responsive. The hostility is un-structured because of lack of expectancy, hope and a sense of self-worth and is ready for random expression. What are we heading into when we organize latently hostile people into power groups that are left to find their own ethical methods and objectives? Will they strive to discover ethical principles to restrain or guide their uses of power? This is a basic question.

It is not my purpose at this point, however, to deal with the issues of community organization and social ethics. I am trying to cope with the nature of the hostility that ultimately tends to energize the behavior patterns of the poor as they are urged— almost required—to adopt the habits and manners of the prosperous.

Conversion Needed

In order for the prosperous to make the larger community open its doors to the poor there must be a conversion of the *prosperity-afflicted mind* that equals in depth the conversion demanded of the *poverty-inflicted mind*. When Jesus remarked that we always have the poor with us, he was speaking in a context that urged people to go ahead with the celebration of other social values even if the problems of the poor had not been solved. But the same context permits us to say that the problems of the poor will never be solved simply by unleashing their latent hostility upon the prosperous and their middle-class value system. The salvation of the *poor who are in poverty* requires a change of the mind-set of the prosperous, and it is entirely possible that this change in mind-set could be the salvation also of the many bored and dissolutely soft people who are prosperous. Change of mind-set would require the prosperous to see in truth that to be prosperous is to be fortunate, but neither superior nor automatically virtuous. Until prosperous Christians realize that they are fortunate beneficiaries of favorable social situations, and that the poor are victims of contrary social circumstances, there is small hope that we will be spared the unleashing of the hostility of the poor against the prosperous. The Economic Opportunity Act demands that the poor leave their poverty and become prosperous. At the same time there is considerable movement toward community organization techniques that lead to the acquisition of social power by the poor. There are enough people in poverty in this country today to upset traditional social values and practices—and possibly they should be upset—but one must ask what will replace them. A potential social revolution is stirring in the souls of the poor, whose suppressed hostilities toward the prosperous are generally not even faintly understood by the latter.

Other kinds of hostility are functioning darkly in the human soul, but in our culture the burgeoning hostility in the souls of the poor is currently being nursed into expression by a vast government program and a budding revolutionary movement called community organization. We may be approaching one of the most interesting social transactions in history, because the poor now realize that they can upset the larger community of the prosperous without coming into it and without conforming to its value system.

It is customary to include in a discussion of the poor some emotionalized appeal for those who suffer poverty. This I have not done because I take it that most of us are capable of pity.

We have spent far too much time feeling sorry for the poor without loving them in their poverty. Hardly anybody finds people in poverty easy to love. We want them to change before we love them, and this brings me to my fourth point.

The Poor Are Unlovely

The poor are unlovely. Poverty is loathsome, and the poor have the smell of poverty on their bodies, on their breath and in their garments. Take anyone blindfolded into a place where the poor are living, and he can tell by the smell how poor they are. Scores of times I have walked into the sanctuary of the First Methodist Church in Schenectady, New York, and with my nostrils detected, even in the darkness, the presence of a poor person hiding or sleeping there—a weary body trying to find shelter from the harshness of the world outside—a world in the hands of those in the realm of prosperity.

Which of us seeks friendship among the poor? Which of us finds an evening delightful in the home of the poverty-stricken? Where do we go to find members for our churches, clubs, status organizations? How do we deal with the ill-fed, ill-housed, ill-clothed people whose teeth are rotted, whose breath is foul and whose stake in American life was forfeited before their birth?

These are the unloved and the unlovely—the objects of special legislation, special community organization and a nation-wide demand that they become other than they are. This is not to deny that the plight of the poor should be improved and poverty wiped forever from the earth. All this should be, but it will never be if we wait until the poor are lovely before we love them.

Love for the unlovely is part of the Christian ethic. Nothing short of a nation-wide surge of love for persons who are poor, not because they are poor but because they are persons; nothing short of a tremendous, nation-wide emergence of deep love between prosperous and poor will save the poor *and* the prosperous.

In the final analysis we are not engaged in a war on poverty. Poverty is not the enemy. The enemy is the socially structured pattern of attitudes in the larger community of the prosperous. The attitudes of the prosperous, more than anything else, make people in poverty stay there as outcasts, ranked as indecent, hostile in deeply sullen ways, hopeless and without high dreams. These are the unlovely, whose redemption waits for love generated in the hearts of the prosperous.

chapter III

WHY DO PEOPLE STAY POOR?

Everyone who knows anything about people in poverty is painfully aware of their stubborn residence in it. It would seem that any person living in poverty would do almost anything to get out of it, but the evidence piles up to the contrary.

Reports come out with regularity, telling us that the family on welfare is now a "third-generation welfare family," and every town or city has its list of men and women who have not been regularly employed and self-supporting since birth. In some sections of the nation it is now natural to classify some people as unemployable. Most of the readers of this book probably would endorse this classification after a few days of intimate association with those so classified. It is not easy to think of illiterate, sick, hopeless people as candidates for any job, and there are millions of persons in this nation whom the prosperous would not allow to mow the lawn or pick up the leaves.

At the same time there is enough work in this country to keep every person in the nation busy day and night. Jobs are not always available, but there is always work to be done. Let us for a moment assume that through some miracle of private and public initiative a vast number of new jobs could be opened up. This is really what the new Office of Economic Opportunity (OEO) is setting out to do. Filthy city streets need to be cleaned, river fronts made fit for living; and our educational and housing needs could employ millions of hands for a long, long time.

Let us assume the possible, which is that enough jobs will be opened up to put every healthy person in position to earn a decent living. Let us assume that jobs will increase family income until it is substantially above the level now used to indicate poverty-bound people. Will the people now in poverty be able to get out of their poverty by this kind of economic boost?

It seems evident that even this kind of economic aid, which is the best there is, will not be enough because people are kept in poverty by factors other than economic needs. People are linked to poverty by certain social characteristics which cannot be changed or eliminated by purely economic means. This is not to say that they can be saved from poverty without economic help. Economic help is absolutely essential, but it is not enough. It is important for Christians to understand this, and it is particularly important to church leaders on the local level. It is very likely that local churches will determine whether the war against poverty will end in victory or defeat for the nation.

We have noted that people stay poor because of the attitudes of the prosperous. The prosperous are not the rich. They are the people who know that they have a continuing part in the larger community prevailing in this nation. The prosperous are the people who can buy on credit more goods than they can readily pay for, and they can spend more money than they should on food, recreation and personal gratifications. The prosperous may not have much money on hand, but they have access to the flow of money, and they dip regularly into its stream, one way or another. In short, the prosperous belong to the club. They feel that they are "in" the main part of society, and they know that they *have* rights even if they do not *own* them, with all installments paid.

The prosperous also tend to think that the poor do not deserve these same rights. I hope to offer proof for the proposition that the prosperous keep the poor in poverty, but it is highly probable that the prosperous will find arguments to remove the sting of the charge. Almost all church people are prosperous even though they do not usually so consider themselves. As often as not, people who spend a lot of money think that they do not have much. Even if some church people have hardly any ready cash they belong to the four-fifths of the nation outside poverty.

Let us ask again the basic question: Why do people stay poor? This question has attracted the interest of foundation-supported specialists, to ascertain answers other than the quick ones given by people anxious and impatient on encountering the poor. These anxious, impatient people tend to say that the poor lack motivation, intelligence, ambition and other desirable qualities. These charges are probably true, but they do not explain the lacks, they only point them out.

Poverty-linked Characteristics

Why does any person remain poor in a society of affluence? Studies now available reveal certain poverty-linked characteristics—if we use the language of Professor Oscar Ornati* of the New School for Social Research. Professor Ornati engaged in an inquiry on behalf of the Twentieth Century Fund and concluded that people remain in poverty because they cannot break the links that chain them to poverty. These links are as follows:

(1) *Old age.* To be old is not to be poor automatically, but if one is old and poor, his chances of getting out of poverty are approximately zero. There are 18,000,000 men and women in the nation past 65 years of age. The Social Security Administration reports that 1,900,000 retired couples (3,800,000 persons) and 5,700,000 unattached retired persons now have incomes substantially beneath the poverty level. This is to say that more than one-half of the people past age sixty-five are in poverty and are there to stay under present conditions.

(2) *Color.* If one is non-white, his chances of being in poverty are increased and his chances of getting out of poverty are definitely reduced.

(3) *Membership in a family headed by a female.* If the father left home for any reason, or if the mother did not get married for some reason, the family's chances of *being* in poverty are definitely increased, and its chances of *remaining* in poverty are increased.

(4) *Membership in a rural family* increases one's chances both of being poor and staying that way, in spite of all one can do.

---

* Professor Ornati's book, *Poverty Amidst Affluence,* may be obtained for $3.75 from Twentieth Century Fund, 41 E. 70th St., New York, N. Y.

(5) If one has *less than eight years of education,* he is probably in poverty to stay.

(6) If the head of a family has only a *part-time job,* the family has a very good chance of being in poverty and of staying there.

Ornati discovered that families with only *one* of the above characteristics had a one-in-three chance of being below the $4,500 income range, which is higher than the prevailing definition of poverty-income for a family of four. However, if a family has *none* of the above poverty-linked characteristics, its chance of having an income under $4,500 is reduced to about one in eight. Which is to say that one's chances of being out of poverty are almost 300 per cent better if he is not linked by the items listed by Ornati.

There is more to the story. *Two* of the above-noted links increase dramatically one's chances of being poor. Actually, combinations of these links increase one's chance of being in poverty to about three out of four. For example, a non-white family with a female as head of the house is virtually condemned to poverty. An aged family living on a farm is likely to have the same fate. An aged Negro family living anywhere is almost certain to be in poverty. So it goes through the combinations.

We should go beyond Ornati's findings to see if we can discover why these poverty-linked characteristics are so effective.

It is my argument that they are effective in keeping people in poverty because the attitudes of the prosperous make them effective. This is a serious charge, both to make and to bear, and the implications for the churches are clear if there is substance to the charge.

Let us look clearly at these links. People of color tend to be poor. There is not one iota of evidence to support the notion that people of color cannot be good workers, capable artisans and socially valuable producers of goods and services. But in spite of their demonstrated economic worth to society whenever they are given a chance, most people of color are poor and will continue apparently to be poor until a change takes place in the attitudes of the prosperous. This is sin at its ugliest and most persistent level because it rests upon the unconscious sense of white-superiority and the ages-long social submission of the colored people, who fear the cost of breaking out into the open to press their legitimate claims. White people think of colored people as inferior, and colored people either have believed them or have feared what it would cost to contradict them. Consequently, the colored remain poor. Often the newly prosperous colored person develops an attitude of superiority more pronounced than the white attitude, thus reinforcing the community attitude of prosperous whites.

We live in a job society. Most jobs pay enough to live on while one works. Few jobs pay enough for saving enough money for retirement, which comes earlier than it used to. Add to this our increased longevity, and there results a problem of considerable magnitude. People cannot help growing old, but this is not really the problem. The problem is that an older person generally is regarded as useless, a little slow, somebody to be gotten out of the way. We retire him, with or without pension, and try to forget him. We also preserve the myth that people should save enough for retirement. This attitude keeps old people in poverty because it prevents the development of intelligent programs that will make possible a home to live in, medical care when needed, and some meaningful way to invest one's older years on behalf of a world needing what older people can share as much as it needs what younger people can give.

Unchristian Attitude

The prevailing attitude toward older people in our society is stupid and unworthy of Christian affirmations about the dignity of personality and the worth of God's creatures. The attitudes of the prosperous generally consent to the proposition that when a person is not able to draw wages from a job in the production of goods or traditional services, the end of his usefulness to society as a whole has arrived. This attitude keeps older people out òf work and in poverty because it short-circuits any plans of private or public enterprise that would put older people into useful and rewarding work. This is *not* to argue that people should be held with their noses to the grindstone until they collapse. It *is* to argue that people can be useful even when old.

Fundamentally, limited conception of the range of useful and rewarding work cripples the contemporary mind and among the prosperous represents a lack of imagination. It has been demonstrated time and again that older people who cannot engage in work essential for production of goods and traditional services are well suited to the performance of tasks currently not being performed at all in our society. Among such jobs might be listed supervision of parks and playgrounds where simple general oversight is all that is needed; the development of mutual-aid programs where the health, recreation and general welfare of older people are involved; and general services to the hospitals, homes, schools and public agencies of the community. At numerous volunteer centers in this nation older people have demonstrated their tremendous capacity to influence and carry forward the general welfare, and it is high time that this energy and capacity be structured into the economy in such a way that older people can continue to participate in the whole life of the community, including the economic. Currently, the attitude of the prosperous supports the practice of "wages until retirement" and after that the pension and social security, if one is lucky enough to have both. If not, then some kind of welfare may supplement whatever one may have. The average Social Security payment to retired people in July, 1965, was $77.53 per month. In January, 1965, 40 per cent of the 2,154,581 retired people receiving Social Security were also on public welfare. Advances since then still do not meet the problem.

What does it mean to go on welfare? Let us take New York City—which is better than most places—as an example. If an individual must have help after age 65, his affairs are carefully scrutinized and he is put on a budget of $21.80 for each 15 days of his life. This covers food, clothing, household supplies and general living expenses. He will receive additional rental allowance to dwell in a place usually unfit for human habitation.

On the national scene conditions are no better, because the average welfare payment for an aged person is $78.51 per month. No wonder the suicide rate for the aged is higher than for any other age group! And why be surprised that 27 per cent of the admissions to mental hospitals are of people past 65 years of age? The nursing homes of the nation are concealed scandals, and one could ask why ministers of churches, who know as much about nursing homes as anyone else, have not raised the national roof in protest.

To be aged and poor is to be condemned to poverty, and one simply cannot avoid being aged in due course of time. Should not every individual, then, arrive at old age with enough resources to see things through neatly until the happy day of his death? How much would be needed to take care of an aged couple, through sickness, weakness and several months of terminal illness? With hospital care costing $200 per week it does not take long to run through an estate. The likelihood is remote that more than a small fraction of the population will, under prevailing circumstances, be self-supporting in old age. Great numbers of the aged will be in poverty until the prosperous have a different attitude toward growing older. Our affluent society has the technology to keep people alive but lacks sufficient decency to let them perform services, for which they receive an economic portion sufficient to keep them out of poverty.

This rather lengthy excursion into the economics of the aged by no means opens up the subject in its full dimension. It serves only to illustrate what is meant by the charge that the attitudes of the prosperous keep the poor in poverty. We have dealt with this in connection with people of color and aged people. Now let us consider how this is true in a family headed by a female. In March, 1964, the Bureau of the Census reported that in 8.6 per cent of the families in this country a female is the head of the household. This is the average for the entire nation. Breaking the figures down into white and non-white families, we find that about 7.5 per cent of the entire white households and 18.5 per cent of the non-white households are headed by females. This does not mean that non-white men are less dependable in family matters. Numerous other factors enter into the formation of households headed by females, one of the most significant being that welfare regulations often require a man to abandon his family if it is to obtain aid from welfare funds. Low wages of colored workers often force colored men to leave their families because welfare support will provide the family a minimum support higher than his wages. More colored men are on low wages than white men in the same category.

All the factors entering into the creation of households headed by females cannot be discussed here, but we should establish the point that when we study that portion of the population living in poverty, we find that a marked proportion lives in households headed by females. This is factual data. All we need do is recognize the phenomenon of the female-headed family as being distinctive of those in poverty.

Poverty in Rural Sections

Now let us look at some of the reasons why people in rural sections are likely to be in poverty.

"The Independent Bankers Association compiled the startling fact that farmers during the period from 1952 to 1962 earned 2.3 per cent less gross farm income than in the 4 worst years of the Depression; also that while national income as a whole increased 100 per cent, net farm income *decreased* 25 per cent. The National Policy Committee on Pockets of Poverty in March, 1964 concluded that the surest way to be poor is to be non-white, live in a rural area, and be the female head of a household or over age 65.

"The United States Department of Agriculture maintains that poverty is twice as prevalent in rural America as in urban

America. While only 30 per cent of our families live in rural areas, they include 46 per cent of the American families with incomes under $3,000.

" 'In 1963,' says economist Leon H. Keyserling, 'the medium income of non-farm families was $7,644, while that of farm families was $4,107. More than 43 per cent of farm families live in poverty, contrasted with 17 per cent of all non-farm families. In 1961, 46 per cent of all farm workers earned less than $5.00 per day, and only 17 per cent earned $9.00 a day or better . . . the average annual money wages of non-migratory farm workers is $340. Even assuming some other sources of income, the plight of these people is tragic.' " [1]

Another poverty-linked characteristic exists in the case of persons who have less than eight years of education. This feature does not need to be discussed at great length. What many prosperous people do not realize is that there are thousands of places in this nation where it is hard to get more than eight years of school experience. There are places in all parts of the United States where classes beyond the eighth grade can be reached only by lengthy travel. However, this is not the main problem. Youths who drop out constitute the big problem, and we do not understand this phenomenon as well as we should if we are to cope with it. We can be sure of one thing: we will not solve the problem by pouring scorn on the drop-outs nor by babying them, either. This is a deep-rooted social phenomenon that probably has any number of causes, and the only statement that can be made at this point is that a person with no more than eight grades of schooling is likely to live out his days in poverty.

Finally, if the head of a family has only a part-time job, all members of the family have a good chance of spending their days in poverty. Add this characteristic to one or two of the others we have mentioned, and there is almost certain condemnation to a life in poverty. The worker who is on a job only

---

[1] Henry A. McCanna, "The Captive Rural Poor," *Information Service* (National Council of Churches, September 11, 1965), Vol. XLIV, No. 14, p. 7. Used by permission.

part-time is often one whose health is limited or whose skills are in seasonal demand. Migrant workers are good examples of the seasonal worker. The food we eat may come to us at a low price because the worker is paid a low wage. The low wage is possible because the worker cannot do other kinds of work. Part-time employment is all that he can obtain and, given the marketing situation, it may be all that the grower thinks he can pay. Similar implications relate to almost all part-time jobs, and a family whose breadwinner and head is on this basis of employment suffers great risk of living out a life in poverty.

Up to this point our discussion has been based on studies coming out in various forms all over the nation. Now let us take a step that will move us a little farther than these studies have done.

Let us ask a simple question that we naturally forget to raise because the evidence from the items we have been discussing seems convincing. Let us ask why the six poverty-linked characteristics are so powerful in their influence over human lives? Do they receive their force from the attitudes prevailing in the community of the prosperous? In some cases it will be immediately clear that this is so, because we have recently, for example, been made keenly aware that people of color have been discriminated against. We have not been made equally aware of our discrimination against older people, families headed by females, rural families left behind by agricultural technology, school dropouts and part-time workers.

The attitudes of the prosperous toward these poverty-linked characteristics are not violent, aggressive and accusative. Hundreds of years ago there was little social disturbance over who the colored people are or their role in society. The attitudes of people were settled. In the same way, the attitudes of the prosperous toward the poverty-linked characteristics are currently settled, quiet and by no means the source of great social agitation and concern. That is why they are so powerful. They are effective because they are unrecognized as existing. As long as these "sleeping" attitudes prevail among the prosperous, the poor under the dominion of these poverty-linked characteristics will be held back from entering the community of the prosperous.

The Economic Opportunity Act and the Office of Economic Opportunity constitute important and necessary social advances in the direction of liberating the poor from the community of poverty, but this liberation cannot possibly take place only through federal economic generosity or education for existing jobs. More powerful than these is the tremendous force for poverty continuance throughout the socially structured and largely unconscious attitudes of the prosperous.

People will never emerge from poverty until the prosperous perform the miracle of making socially acceptable the features now linking people to poverty, so that those who are poor will "belong" with the prosperous. This is a matter of attitudes, and the Christian Church is committed to dealing with attitudes.

The attitudes of the Good Samaritan made it possible for him to get down into a ditch by the side of a man who was unable to manage a journey well enough to avoid being beaten up by thugs. This accomplishment on the part of the Samaritan was not accidental. To be socially redemptive is no accident, and it begins with having redemptive attitudes toward people in a ditch, which is exactly where the poor are today.

chapter IV

WHY RELIEF AND WELFARE FAIL

Relief and welfare programs offer refuge from starvation, exposure and gross neglect but they fail to bring people out of poverty. Poverty is a social predicament and produces a subculture within which poor people live and move and have their being. Confined by their poverty-linked characteristics to this ghetto, they are relieved of many of the pains that would afflict them if they did not receive relief funds and welfare services. But we know by now that these programs do not bring the poor out of poverty into prosperity.

The statistics of people locked in poverty are overwhelming, and have been staring us in the face for at least the 20 years since 1945, when we first became capable as a nation of putting an end to poverty for every citizen. During this 20-year period (1945-1965) the portion of the population in poverty has remained about the same, when measurements include the numerous adjustments that have to be made for general social and economic advances for the society as a whole. What this means is that the poorest in this nation may not seem so poor when compared to the poorest of a century ago, or when contrasted with the poorest of some less fortunate nation, but they are horribly poor when compared to the 80 per cent who are prosperous.

No matter how we compare the present with the past we have had persistent poverty in the nation, and to a very large extent it involves generation after generation of the same families. In New York City alone it was reported, near the close of 1964, that 500,000 people were on welfare and that a heavy proportion of these were in their third generation as welfare recipients. It was further noted that the number was being increased at the rate of 6,000 per month, but among these a heavy portion were

47

already welfare dependents of some state or county before arriving in New York, which does not have a time requirement of residence before one is eligible for relief and welfare benefits.

Statistics become dull, and we shall not labor the point to prove that descendants of people on relief and welfare tend also to be poor. In the previous chapter we have discussed why this is so: people are poverty-linked by social characteristics that draw their power from the attitudes of the prosperous.

Why do not people in poverty make the adjustments necessary to get into the community of the prosperous and qualify for a life of self-support and prosperity? This is a good question. Let us face it and see what we learn.

Color of skin is a major link to the life of poverty. What can one do about the color of one's skin? Being old is a poverty-linked characteristic. Can one avoid growing older? Having a female at the head of one's family links one to poverty. This can be changed, of course, but how hard is this to do if there are three or four children in the house? Living in a rural section links one to poverty. This can be changed by moving to a city, if one has the money to pack up, travel, rent an apartment and live long enough to find a job that may not be eagerly waiting for the probably limited skills of the bread-winner. If one has only eight years or less of school experience, this can be remedied by entering a school to seek more education. Who supports the family while this is being done, and how easy is it to go back to school when one is several years older than the rest of the class? Finally, the part-time worker is linked to poverty. A full-time job would be welcome, indeed. But what if the worker is on part-time because of poor health, seasonal needs or some other limiting factor?

It seems clear that even if those in poverty wanted to meet the expectations of the prosperous and fit into their world of values in order to crawl out of poverty, they would not be able to do so. They are victims of powerful social forces over which they have little or no control. Although our tradition of mercy ministers to suffering and pain, relief and welfare fail because we lack the social attitudes that lead us to pay attention to the social circumstances inflicting the pain of poverty.

Relief programs and welfare services currently in operation are designed to bind up the wounds of individuals and comfort, somehow, the miseries of families. These programs and services represent a tremendous advance over the neglects of yesterday. It is to the credit of Christian people that they have been the first to see the need for charity, and as a result of Christian efforts all kinds of welfare services were invented to meet the urgent needs of persons and families suffering from the miseries only those in poverty can understand. In a certain sense, Christian people through their churches took pride in person-to-person relationships whereby the prosperous shared their good things with the poor. Offerings were taken to buy good things to send to the poor. Hospitals were built, and mission outposts were established with great satisfaction. While the prosperous went on their joyous way in prosperity, the miserable poor continued in poverty.

New Ministry

After the First World War, a layman's inquiry dealing with Christian missions after a century of world-wide effort showed a strong inclination away from conversion of the "heathen" to a ministry of relief and welfare. Here is only one suggestive quotation from the report:

"We believe the time has come to set the educational and other philanthropic aspects of mission work free from organized responsibility to the work of conscious and direct evangelism. We must work with greater faith in invisible successes, be willing to give largely without any preaching, to cooperate wholeheartedly with non-Christian agencies for social improvement, and to foster the initiative of (others) in defining the ways in which we shall be invited to help." [1]

It is indeed interesting to find these same thoughts developed

---

[1] *Re-Thinking Missions, A Layman's Inquiry After One Hundred Years* (New York: Harper and Brothers, 1932), p. 326. Used by permission.

at length in Harvey Cox's *The Secular City,* as though they had never been thought of before. This indicates how slow we are to come to the truth. It is even more surprising to recall that even before *Re-Thinking Missions* was written, Walter Rauschenbusch * had preached the same message with a devout and disturbing passion.

Adding all this, we end with a discovery of the Old Testament prophets and the New Testament saints who stoutly insist that true religion is not limited to prayers and hymn singing in the church but only begins there. True religion exists only when the worshiper goes into the world to serve God through service to his *nearest* fellow man, not the one far enough away to be served by a few dollars and who can be forgotten in a few minutes. This shift of mission strategy, from that of converting the "heathen" to a ministry of relief and welfare, gathered momentum as the cybernetic or technological revolution began to pour a greater and greater volume of goods out of the American industrial cornucopia. This might have been predicted, because Christian people are conditioned to feel guilty if they have too much while others have too little—and this applies forcefully to economic goods. It also includes other social goods. Perhaps one of the truly unique qualities of Christianity is its ability to promote a sense of guilt among its adherents when they feel they have too much of a good thing and others have too little.

In any case, the world movement of Christianity will stand in history as a major effort on the part of Christian people to give relief and welfare to people whose lives are chained to poverty at a time when prosperity apparently was unavoidable for many others in a few nations of the Western world.

The pity of it is that welfare and relief did not work. They did not work because they could not. Perhaps it would be better to say that if the goal of relief and welfare programs was to bring people out of poverty into the community of the pros-

---

* Rauschenbusch, Walter (1861-1918). American Baptist clergyman, leader in social interpretation and application of Christianity.

perous, the goal was not reached. It may be that the goal was the relief from suffering of the few persons who could be reached. If that *was* the goal, it worked insofar as it reached some persons and relieved them of some of their misery for a few hours.

Christianity as a world movement has manifested a limited viewpoint in this regard, at least up to the present. It has tried to meet the needs of persons without facing the nature of the social systems that produce, rather than relieve, human needs. The major reason why Christianity is now on the defensive as it confronts communism is because there has been a traditional reluctance of Christianity as a world movement to become involved in structuring social changes. This is to say that for the past several centuries Christianity has been more inclined to give merciful relief and welfare than it has been to engage in hardheaded analysis of social reality and to follow up the analysis by grappling with social systems.

Alfred Cobban, the distinguished historian of the University of London, has taken note of this failure in his evaluation of the period we call the Age of Enlightenment, which covered the seventeenth and eighteenth centuries. This was the so-called Age of Reason, but it was also characterized by a genuine concern for corrections of the social systems that inflicted pain upon persons. Cobban notes that pain has been used in the past as a means of control by ecclesiastical systems, and the Inquisition with its tortures is a case in point. For a time pain was then used as a means of judicial procedure, and the extraction of confessions by inflicting pain was more or less routine until fairly recently. At the present time the infliction of pain is by political systems, and by this Cobban means socio-economic systems, because that is precisely what political systems are. This is to say that pain is inflicted in our time, not by cruel persons who are cruel to other persons but by merciful persons whose systems just happen to be cruelty-inflicting systems.

Personal vs. Community Ideals

In 1932 Reinhold Niebuhr wrote what may be the most important of his long and distinguished list of books. It was the famous *Moral Man and Immoral Society*. His thesis in that book is that the tragedy of the human spirit is that the ideals of persons cannot become the practices of the community. Thus, the merciful man will inevitably find that his social systems involve him in unmerciful acts. Niebuhr was writing in an hour of dreadful depression. A World War had been followed by a League of Nations that was no sooner born than strangled. Events were now evolving into another World War which could be seen by discerning minds even in 1932. No wonder Niebuhr took a pessimistic view of society, although he manifested a relatively optimistic view of individuals.

In any case, Niebuhr, following a long list of distinguished scholars, took note of what Cobban holds as a major issue: good people may do evil things because the system of society within which they operate is the ultimate force over the lives of their neighbors, both prosperous and poor.

The reluctance of the Christian Church to tackle the social systems of our time should be understood. When we look over our shoulders at the past, we see what it meant for the Church to try to take the role of the state. The Church did no better in developing systems that took care of human needs than the state had done. In some instances the worst periods of history are those in which the Church had the most power over social systems and practices. John Wesley seemed to recognize this. He had the Reformation behind him and at the same time he lived in a situation where identification of the Church and the state endangered, as he saw it, the essential freedom of the religious experience. Concerned for the vitality of a fully free religious experience, he shunned too close an identification of the Church with the state, and he even tended to steer clear of too much dominion of the Church over religious experience itself.

The Reformation pulled the Church out into a field where it

was divorced from the prevailing ecclesiastical-social system, but Wesley's influence pulled the individual out of the Church by making the "warm heart" a final test of religious truth. It should be emphasized that Wesley did this neither deliberately nor directly, but those who were influenced by Wesley ultimately did it. Sidney Mead traces this in his book, *The Lively Experiment*. This is one of the more important books of this decade because it shows how Methodists exerted strong support of personal piety with correspondingly strong support of an attitude which said, "Leave the social systems alone."

This takes a good many Methodists of our time by surprise, because justifiable pride is taken in the fact that the Methodist Social Creed adopted in 1907 was the first to be adopted by any denomination and offered a basic pattern for the one adopted later by the (then) Federal Council of Churches. Yet it must be accepted as an historical truth that Methodists have not by tradition been greatly concerned with social systems. This has been demonstrated by Professor Richard M. Cameron in *Methodism and Society in Historical Perspectives*, a book in the MESTA (Methodist Social Thought and Action) series published as a project of the Methodist Board of Christian Social Concerns.

Methodists are sufficiently representative of the population in this respect for us to generalize with some assurance that Christian people as a whole have been inclined for a couple of centuries to think that religion should not meddle in politics. Or if Christians do, they should do it on a strictly personal basis and avoid having the church involved as an institution.

This attitude assumes that society can be influenced by individuals, as it no doubt can be, provided the individual finds some way of expressing his interests by means of some kind of institution or organization. Individuals operating alone are helpless, whether they have billions of dollars or are in poverty. In a society of institutions the individual must find his effective expression of interest through institutions.

But the Christian churches have not faced the institutions of our time because to do this would involve the institutional church in great risks.

We will return to this issue in a later chapter, but mention of this problem has to be made at this point because Christian people are now involved in a great disillusionment. Their hope that they might help those in poverty has been dashed, and we need now to face in full dimension why relief and welfare have failed and how this failure is having its impact upon our mission in the world today. The Christian mission, which has been based in part upon the proposition that merciful works would redeem societies, has been proved to have a doubtful foundation. Communism repudiates the concept of relief and welfare in favor of a system that promises to make these unnecessary. This tremendous promise has elements of the extravagant over-promises which may end up in widely-spread bitterness and disillusionment in communist nations, but the clear claim of communism that it has no room for relief and welfare programs is taken seriously by other nations.

On the level of world mission the administration of relief and welfare by Christians has been a monument to the Christian spirit of mercy and compassion. Hundreds of Christians in the United States have made personal sacrifices of money to minister to the needs of people. After more than a century of compassionate ministry in relief and welfare programs it is something of a shock to us to discover that the very people we have loved and tried to serve are not satisfied with what we have done. With increasing energy they are saying to us that they want more than relief and welfare services.

What is the *more* they want? The Congo provides a vivid example. The *more* that was passionately desired in the Congo was a different system of social transactions. This included the removal of Belgium's control and the end of ownership of natural resources by other than Congolese. It meant the structuring of a new society in the shape of Congolese hopes, and the reason for the bloody and confused internal struggle after the Belgians pulled out was the conflict among various Congolese leaders on how the social system should be shaped and who should control it.

Shift in Work

In the United States there is a similar shift in programs. Methodist work in both cities and rural sections is moving its base from familiar relief and welfare services. A good example is found in the more than 100 community centers administered by the National Division of the Methodist Board of Missions. These are located mainly in cities, and the focus of their work has shifted radically in the past few years. There is a strong trend toward making community centers into agents of social change, and some of them have already installed full-time workers who are specialists in community organization. This is in vivid contrast to the community center as a place where people go to receive relief or welfare services. The new community center is much more concerned with the correction of the social system than with the relief of individual pain and family misery, although it does not ignore these afflictions. It simply does not believe that treating the symptoms of social malady is the end of its responsibility.

In all mission work within the United States there is a general movement away from relief and welfare and toward reconstruction of social procedure. Instead of supporting individuals and agencies engaged in social welfare, Methodists are moving toward the service of individuals and agencies capable of producing social change. But more of this in a later chapter.

It has been our purpose in this chapter to show as clearly as we can that relief and welfare programs fail to bring people out of poverty because they do not sever the links that chain people in the ghetto of poverty. *Expenditure of multi-millions of dollars on relief and welfare programs is like feeding and caring for prisoners chained in a dark, damp prison cell while at the same time expecting them to get out into the open to earn their own livelihood.*

How have we been so misled as to think that relief and welfare would bring people out of poverty? Two situations have blinded us. First, we have not had knowledge. The sociology of poverty is a fairly new field, and lack of knowledge concerning it has been a severe handicap. Until the science of cybernetics opened up the prospect that economic needs could be met—provided the size of the population did not increase too greatly—there was no pressing incentive to find out why people tend to remain in poverty even when surrounded by a community of prosperity. When it became apparent that, given a certain degree of population stability, production of goods could be increased enough to meet all basic needs of all citizens, the reason for persistent poverty in certain sectors of our society became more interesting. When a question becomes interesting people go for the answers. The fact that poverty tends to persist in generation after generation of the same family became of interest in a high-production economy which can use more consumers. Poor people are not good consumers. Our lack of knowledge about why people stay poor has been partly overcome, thanks to the desire for them to be better consumers.

Second, we have been blinded to the real causes of persistent poverty because the *symptom* of poverty—lack of economic goods—is so vivid we have thought that the *cause* of poverty was this lack. At first glance it would seem that people without economic goods could be relieved of poverty if they could be supplied with economic goods. No doubt it is a relief to receive economic goods when kitchen shelves are empty, lights are cut off, and the landlord is serving an eviction notice. It is also a relief for a person with a brain injury to be given a pain-relieving drug. It is part of our humanity that we wish to relieve people of their pain. Relief and welfare programs? Yes! As a cure? No!

Returning to the main point in this chapter, we find it definite that relief and welfare programs *do* relieve pain caused by economic deprivation. As long as there are people there will be need for relief and welfare programs because a proportion of the population will always suffer a certain amount of economic lack.

When it comes to whether or not relief and welfare projects bring people out of poverty, the answer is an emphatic *"no,"* because relief and welfare programs are not designed to get at the basic causes of poverty, causes not economic but social. It is essential that this be understood if the current war against poverty is not to lead the American public down a bitter, expensive road toward ultimate disillusionment. If we end up a generation later with the same portion of the population in poverty as now, our national spirit will be sick with disappointment, and the prosperous will develop a new hostility toward those in poverty. It is an obligation of Christians to see that this does not happen.

chapter V

HOW CAN POVERTY BE BANISHED?

No sooner had the war against poverty been declared than the slogans began to appear. The one most frequently heard was, "Only the poor can win the war against poverty." This sounds good if you say it quickly. It puts the entire responsibility upon the poor, which is exactly where the prosperous have tended to put it all along.

This slogan was welcomed in political circles, especially in big cities. Poor people vote, and there are enough of them in the larger cities to become a major political bloc if they can be gotten into line. The slogan that victory in the war against poverty would be gained only if the poor won it gave rise to the belief that programs designed to bring people out of poverty would have leaders who were themselves in poverty. This sounds great. Absolutely wonderful! It has a generous note and rings with righteousness because it says that the poor can actually come out of poverty into prosperity—even with their own leadership.

To be perfectly fair, there is a certain amount of truth in the slogan. That is what makes it ring so grandly. Those in poverty are people, and they do have a stake in society. Their viewpoints are worth hearing and their values have a right to be presented for public consideration. Certainly it would be a short-sighted society that denied leadership openings to any particular segment of its body. This much needs to be admitted. But to say that only the poor can win the war against poverty is to indulge in nonsense. Everyone will be needed to win that war, and if we win it, there can be no tug-of-war between parties. It will be a long, hard, anguished pull because we are not dealing merely with economic factors but mainly with the attitudes of the prosperous. These attitudes preserve and give social force to the links forging the chain to hold the poor in poverty. When we deal with attitudes (whether of the prosperous or of the poor) we need the help of everyone, because social attitudes have roots, reasons, arguments, rationalizations, theologies and emotions galore to sustain them.

The Road

In its May, 1965, issue the *Scientific American* published an excellent article in which Alexander H. Leighton reported for his colleagues working in the Cornell Program in Social Psychiatry. Starting in 1949 this group studied a community that had suffered economic collapse soon after 1900 when the building of wooden ships ended. The community is disguised, being called simply the *Road*.

The *Road* consisted of 118 people living in 20 houses, with 66 of the residents being 21 years of age. Perhaps you can visualize the little community, with its small, cramped dwellings separated by fields and woods from other communities. Certain kinds of government relief and welfare come into the community. If you go to surrounding communities and ask about the people living in the *Road*, you are almost invariably told that the people who live there are mentally retarded.

Dr. Leighton and his colleagues began their study by attempting to discover whether or not the people of the *Road* were really retarded. They found that the *Road* children were like the children of neighboring communities. They showed the same mental range, from stupidity to better-than-average intelligence.

Once it was established that the residents were of average intelligence other examinations were in order. The poverty of the people was easy to see because it was everywhere. The educational level was very low, nominally the fourth or fifth grade for the average adult, and with eight adults being unable to read or write. There was a prevalence of broken marriages and family strife, with consequent isolation of individuals from each other even within family circles. The families were even more isolated in their relationships with each other. The only community organization was the church, but the people rarely attended its functions.

Informal organization such as hunting for the men or house-to-house visiting for the women existed, but there was no real community leadership. "The *Road* was, in short, not really a community but a neighborhood based on exclusion." What this means is that the neighboring communities expected the *Road* people to stay in their place. Dr. Leighton writes:

"Attitudes of this kind put innumerable limitations on the people of the 'Road,' making it difficult for them to obtain work, form friendships, and find mates. The mates were mostly from similarly depressed areas and so tended to perpetuate the character of the 'Road' "[1] In other words, the attitudes of the prosperous had put the people of the *Road* into a separate community and closed all ports of entry into the community of the prosperous. This had happened although the people of the *Road* were as intelligent as those who had excluded them. And it had happened without deliberate intention on the part of the surrounding community. This pattern of relationships is developed not only in connection with the people of the *Road*. This happens in regions, nations, and on a world-wide scale. The poor become the despised, the rejected and the poverty-linked, and have little or no control over their fate. They are condemned by the attitudes of the prosperous to live in poverty.

There is more to the story of the *Road*. Dr. Leighton contrasts the value system of the people of the *Road* with that in surrounding communities. A value system is composed of that which individuals say they treasure, such as truth, mercy, beauty, family stability, or education.

"Although most of the values found in the larger society were also evident on the *Road*, expressions of them by *Road* residents were comparatively pale and lacking in commitment. An example was the merely nominal Catholicism of the *Road* people. In addition the people voiced strong sentiments of self-disparagement, mistrust of each other, and mistrust of outsiders, particularly those in positions of authority. Work was regarded as virtueless—a necessary evil to be avoided when possible. The people showed little by way of foresight. They tended to regard the future as uncontrollable, an attitude reflected by the fact that most of them thought the best thing to do with a dollar was to spend it at once, because only in that way could they be assured of getting full use of it." [2]

It is not possible to go into all the detail of this important research, which does so much to support the argument of this book, but let us note what the researchers and others did about it, because the real question we face is how to win the war against poverty.

It was decided that several things should be tried. Although these can be listed in a few words it should not therefore be assumed that they can be put into operation with a twist of the wrist. At the top of the list were:

(1) The introduction of social organization and social values through the development of leadership. This would tend to change the conditions which found the people generally isolated from each other even in the family group.

(2) Education for everyone. This would cope with the attitudes of the people on the *Road* and help them become more able to move with some self-confidence in other communities.

(3) Improved economic opportunity.

The project of "*Road*-help" began with a battery-driven motion picture projector that led to the *Road's* desire for a power line that the people had to help install, and goes from level to level, with ups and downs, but with gradual changes in the whole community. Men were more steadily employed; women more involved in community life. The "disappearance" of the children of the *Road* occurred as they quickly identified with children of the other communities in the consolidated school.

[2] *Op. cit.,* pp. 23-24.

Dr. Leighton and his colleagues draw many definite conclusions, but let us mention only the main generalization in his own words:

"Clearly, increased economic opportunity will not be enough to bring about a turn for the better in a disintegrated community, although such opportunities are essential to the process. What is needed in addition to them is the development of patterns of social functioning: leadership and follower-ship and practice in acting together cooperatively. In other words, it is necessary that the offers of better education and of training in marketable skills go hand in hand with help in *learning the elements of human relations.*" [3]

All this sounds neat and easy. There is some danger that we may say to ourselves, "This is the way to eliminate poverty. Send a research team to every *Road* situation in the United States and in fifteen years we will have won the war." There is *some* value in saying this because by doing so we admit that nothing inside the *Road* would have been enough to change the *Road's* people. What led them to change was the presence of people who came from the world of the prosperous to live with them, be one of them, share with them and accept them.

Dr. Leighton does not make a big point of it, but the project he describes really rested upon a few people who came into the community of the *Road* to prove in the flesh that at least a few persons from the world of the prosperous could accept the people of the *Road*. Those who came brought with them attitudes and plans based on the hope that a better tomorrow was possible for every individual in the *Road*. In particular, two teachers in the story of the *Road* remind us of disciples of the Man of Galilee.

Scores of research projects have come to a conclusion similar to the one reached after the sixteen-year study of the *Road*. In general these projects tell us that poverty can be banished when the attitudes of the prosperous are such that the poor are provided with ports of entry into the community of the prosperous.

---

[3] *Op. cit.*, p. 27. (*Underlining* mine. J.E.C.)

These ports of entry open when the poor are recognized as intelligent and capable of social organization and when they are aided by a little leadership training, and at the same time are stimulated to share in educational opportunities that lead into jobs offering some stability of employment.

Office of Economic Opportunity

When the Economic Opportunity Act was passed by Congress in 1964, it provided for the establishment of the Office of Economic Opportunity. In a burst of energy projects were launched for every age group. Headstart programs to help preschool children in poverty were in full swing by July, 1965. These were intended to insure that these children would not be too far behind their prosperous counterparts when they reached formal school age. Youth Corps opportunities of various kinds were established, and cities as well as rural areas stretched out their hands for funds from the federal coffer. Complaints were numerous that the war against poverty was falling into hands that would busily employ the funds for political ends, but for the most part the nation seemed happy with the prospect that somehow or other the one-fifth of a nation in poverty would be changed into people of prosperity. There has never been any doubt that the American people believe that poverty is a bad thing. Here was a chance to get rid of it.

Only a few voices uttered the criticism that there was nothing really new in the programs designed to end poverty in the United States. There were recollections of the CCC (Civilian Conservation Camps) and the WPA (Work Progress Administration)—which did yeoman service in the Great Depression of the 1930's—without much consideration of whether or not those programs had served as bridges leading from the community of poverty into the community of prosperity. Who really knows what happened to the people in those projects? Who knows what would have happened to them if those projects had never been?

In any case, the war against poverty has a new element in it. There has been a very fruitful period of writing by economists with a sociological interest. Among these Kenneth Galbraith attracted the earliest and most lively notice. In his book, *The Affluent Society,* he said:

"The myopic preoccupation with production and material investment has diverted our attention from the more urgent questions of how we are employing our resources and, in particular, from the great need and opportunity for *investing in persons.*" [4]

Economists with an interest in sociology seemed to arouse the students of sociology, and a surge of interest developed in how to win the war against poverty. To a surprising degree the sociologists were in agreement with the general proposition that the war cannot be merely an economic action. The real enemy is not poverty (which is a symptom) but certain social features that persist because the prosperous have attitudes that make them persist. These attitudes are listed in Chapter Two of this book and discussed at some length in Chapter Three.

At least one noted sociologist took the position that the war against poverty could be won in a generation if enough energy and possibility for development of intelligence were given to small children, beginning as early as the age of three. Oscar Ornati of the New School for Social Research strongly supported this position on the ground that the poverty-linked characteristics he had found in his studies could be more quickly and effectively broken up if the very young child could be provided with a self-image that more or less helped him identify himself with the community of the prosperous. In other words, Ornati favored bringing the child into the community of the prosperous before he identified himself completely with those in poverty.

During this ferment something began to show up in the American social pattern. While Congress had passed a measure that carried with it a large sum of money, local communities

---

[4] Kenneth Galbraith. *The Affluent Society* (Boston: Houghton Mifflin Co., 1958), p. 332. Used by permission. (*Underlining* mine. J.E.C.)

did not have adequate leadership to put the measures into operation. The war against poverty had been planned on the assumption that each community would wage the war in its own way, excepting for the exceedingly general provisions that certain standards and procedures had to be met. It is probably fair to say that the Economic Opportunity Act gave more freedom for the development of local initiative than any other federal program ever before voted by Congress.

Resources of the Church

Somewhat to the surprise of those who had been berating the institutional church for its many shortcomings, it developed that the churches were rich with people who had acquired certain skills necessary for community organization. Skills for planning, group decision-making and other essential ingredients of community action were often found in the churches when they did not exist anywhere else. Undoubtedly the lamentations of Peter L. Berger in his book, *The Noise of Solemn Assemblies,* have some validity. His argument that the Christian may often have to serve Christ outside the established church no doubt has a real bearing in many cases and needs our most attentive ear. The "woe upon woe" directed against the captive church in surburbia is rough to hear, but listening does not hurt. We might learn something.

On the other hand, the established church may have been doing something in its "captivity" that will prove to have value. While both laymen and clergy may have been guilty to a certain extent of playing organizational games in the institutionalized church, they have also been acquiring skills that many persons outside the church did not have when the Economic Opportunity Act made it possible for local communities to act.

This is ironic, but history is laden with interesting ironies. Is it possible that the big, fat, lazy institution of the church—with its baffling demands for organizational skills that have been the bane of the clergy and the happy-hunting-ground of certain types of laymen—has been a training field for the kind of individual now needed to win the war against poverty and deal with a highly complex society? This may be true in some measure because in city after city those able to get projects started often were clergy and laymen whose long church-related experience in dealing with organizational procedures and group decision-making proved to be a rare and needed community skill.

In any case the churches now occupy the best strategic position they have held in this century for proving false the serious charges laid against them in recent years. The charge that the churches are not really relevant to society has to be taken seriously, and the supporting evidence is heavy. There are, however, two reasons why the churches are in such good position to prove the charges false. First, as noted above, there are in the churches individuals whose skills in organizational enterprise are amazingly well developed when compared to those of persons who have not had years of experience inside an organized institution. It takes years to learn how to conduct a simple business meeting, but most churches have any number of members who can do it without flicking an eyelash. Second, the churches traditionally are committed to dealing with attitudes, and this is the center of the war against poverty.

Furthermore, the organizational skills acquired by church members (almost without their realizing it) are held by persons whose attitudes are the ones keeping the poor in poverty. Poverty can be banished if we achieve a change in the attitudes of the prosperous, but the only successful way known to change the attitude of a person is through involvement in an experience which in and of itself wipes out the old attitude while the new one takes over.

Here is indeed a rare combination. One might almost say that God produced this rare combination of needed organizational skills and attitudes in need of conversion. What an opportunity for the church!

Poverty can be banished. We have the economic power

through increased productive capacity now possible with the computer and the cybernetic revolution. What we lack is attitudes that will break up the poverty-link system that binds the poor perpetually in poverty. It is in this realm that the churches have their greatest opportunity for a renewal of their traditional mission. The Lord of the Church addressed his first audience with a proclamation that he had come to "preach good news to the poor." The good news to the poor in our time will be that the prosperous love them as they are: colored, unemployed, uneducated, unmarried (quite often) but parents, households headed by females, with all that this implies, as well as all the other implications of the six links that should not have the power to chain the poor in poverty. If the prosperous can be converted to love the poor without waiting until the poor have achieved all the social characteristics of the prosperous, the war against poverty will be won.

chapter VI

THE CONVERSION OF THE PROSPEROUS

To be prosperous it is not necessary to have cash in one's pocket. One can have unpaid and overdue bills galore and still be prosperous. Although it is unlikely to occur very often, a person can be almost destitute of material belongings and still be prosperous. Thoreau beside Walden Pond was not in poverty, but he had few possessions. Prosperous people are those with enough education, social freedom and general access to the larger society to know that they can share in it to the extent of their skills or desires.

A novelist may decide to forego the income he could receive from teaching school in order to be free to write on his own schedule. As a result he may have a small income but he is prosperous in the sense that he has made a choice about his role in the economy. A businessman may make several bad decisions in a row and end up without a cent to his name, but he is still prosperous in that he can begin all over again or at least can get a job and continue to have a share in the economy through exercise of the skills, freedoms and motivations that he possesses. He is prosperous because he is prosperity-linked by his family and his social and personality traits.

Most people in prosperity are about as responsible for their good fortune as are people in poverty for their bad fortune. Neither group should be condemned for its mode of existence. Nor should we go to the other extreme and say that no person can do anything at all about his existence. Discussion of the prosperous and the poor should begin and proceed in the admission that each of us belongs, to a large extent, to the community into which we were born. If this is true in politics, religion and education, it is true also in economic matters. Whether we like it or not, the power of economic factors beyond our control and able to determine the nature of our lives is great.

Prosperous people, especially in the United States, are generous with cash. One of the reasons the Christian churches in the United States have flourished and become an "establishment"—which is arousing all kinds of criticism from the ranks of Christians both inside and outside the church—is the steady supply of cash for buildings and programs. As the American income has soared, the proportion of cash-after-taxes being given to the churches has leveled off somewhat, but the record is impressive. The generosity of the American people in response to campaigns, drives and crusades for everything from Save-the-Children to Save-the-Birds is phenomenal. This has to be explained, and although the explanation I am about to offer will arouse certain protests, it should be examined for what it is worth.

Guilt from Prosperity

In a word, prosperous Americans probably are generous because they feel guilty about being prosperous. Not everyone who came to this land of promise was able to make the grade, because it was a rough land to conquer. An agricultural economy followed quickly upon the heels of a wilderness economy, and no sooner was agriculture established than industrialism supplanted it as the main avenue to prosperity. Now the industrial economy is being rivaled by the computer-service economy, with more than half the new jobs since 1957 being created outside the production-distribution-sales area. All this means that we have always been a nation of rapid transition with a continuing awareness of the precarious nature of economic life. Therefore, when we realize how fortunate are most of us, we sit at our tables laden with good things and engage in a ritualistic mention of those "less fortunate than we." That is, we do this if the minister is present or if the day is some special holiday.

The comfortable factor in the feeling of guilt arising from our knowing that we are prosperous and that many others are not is revealed in the way we have found to relieve our guilt. We make a contribution. That is all there is to it. For a long time we could make a contribution to a mission far, far away, and when we carved the turkey of the prosperous we knew in our hearts that we were right—right with God, right with the Holy Church and right with the poor heathen. We had done all we knew to do, and what we had done was good. Out of our sense of guilt came the resources to found missions where teaching, preaching, healing and a certain amount of agricultural and industrial skill were introduced in places untouched before. Guilty feelings are the forces that motivate us to seek and, it is hoped, to find the good life.

Goal of Psychiatry

The contemporary concern of psychiatry with guilty feelings has often been misunderstood, sometimes by psychiatrists themselves. To feel guilty about something for which one has no responsibility might be considered a neurotic form of guilt, and a person can become ill enough from guilt feelings that are justified, let alone those which may not be justified. On the other hand, to feel guilty about nothing is to be without moral vitality. Some popular representations of psychiatry portray the goal of personality as relief from *any* feelings of guilt. Actually, it is the goal of psychiatry to help the troubled person face up to the real nature of what lies within, behind and in front of his feelings of guilt. Psychiatry really says to the guilty person, "Come, now, let us reason together."

The main lesson we have learned from psychiatry is that guilt makes us ill when for any reason we refuse to face all the realities that can be uncovered in connection with our guilt feelings. Attempting to cover up guilty feelings with senseless activity and overindulgence in sensual enterprises is part of the mood of the times, but the attempt does not seem successful. Nor are we successful in covering up our guilt feelings with works of generosity. We tend to feel as guilty after we have paid our tithe (or considerably less!) as we did before the offertory.

Among the more interesting recent discussions of this feature of the Christian's life is Herbert Fingarette's book, *The Self in Transformation,* which goes further toward facing this problem than psychiatrists and counselors have generally tended to go. After a careful examination of the conversion experience, not only in Christianity but also in other religions—especially Buddhism—Fingarette concludes that the experience begins with guilt and is followed by a search for the reality promoting the guilt. This search may be agonizing in its difficulties and may demand a quality of self-honesty beyond the ability of the individual alone. At this point the rituals, the ministrations of priest or prophet, as well as the use of symbols of various kinds, will enable the individual gradually to face the truth of his own self-responsibility. *At the point where the individual accepts personal responsibility for that which causes the feelings of guilt there comes a transformation of the self.*

It is not the purpose of this book to present a full development of how, in order to reinforce the conversion, this self-transformation then draws upon its available reservoir of ideas about God and the nature of the universe and the authority of sacred writings and social values to reinforce the conversion. It is enough for our purposes to show that the basic ingredient of personality transformation (which certainly has direct bearing upon social transformations of any kind) is a sense of guilt connected to reality and ultimately accepted as a personal responsibility, if that is what reality requires. In other words, when we come to the truth about ourselves and accept what it says to us, we are freed of crippling guilt, and the self-in-trouble becomes the self-redeemed.

The process is never completed. If we are truly alive to the meaning of our existence, we go through life in a rising series of movement from guilt to guilt, from transformation to transformation. Christians should be expert at recognizing the nature of guilt and should think of local congregations as communities gathered to deal with individual and collective guilt by continuing encouragement of every kind to face the realities of existence, in order that guilt might serve its true and noble function, which is to lead us through the humanity of Jesus Christ, the Lord of the Church, to God, the Author and Finisher of our destiny.

This we have not thus far been able to do in relation to troubled souls abiding in prosperity while our brothers and sisters grovel in miserable poverty. We have tried almost everything in order to rid ourselves of guilt. We have projected our guilt upon the poor and have called them shiftless, indifferent, lacking in motivation, and so forth. We have treated ourselves to the narcotic comfort of generosity that requires going no further than parting with a very small portion of our disposable income. The climax demonstrating the enormous size of our national guilt was the passing of the Economic Opportunity Act. The first year's budget was set at about $1,000,000,000 which amounts to a paltry $28.50 per year for each of the 35,000,000 persons in poverty. Professor Seymour Melman of Columbia University noted at the time that the government of India with its awful poverty is spending half that much in an effort to alleviate poverty in that nation.

I am concerned here not with the number of dollars but with the amount of relief from guilt brought to the American people by the Economic Opportunity Act. This is cheaper for the prosperous than is psychiatry. Adoption of the Economic Opportunity Act also provided a good opportunity for those who like to project their guilt to pour out a new line of vituperation upon not only the poor but also the Congress. On the whole, the mid-point of 1965 found the American people less painfully guilty because they had found a way on a national scale to do what they had been doing all along on a voluntary and private scale—that is, parting with a little money in the hope that this would bring the poor out of poverty so that we could proceed with our main business—the producing, selling and consuming of more goods.

From the point of view of the Christian Church and its mission to human need, the net effect of the Economic Opportunity Act was partly negative. Although it relieved for a time the deep sense of guilt some Christians were beginning to have concerning those in poverty, it put off into the future any prospect that the guilt would lead, in due course of time, to the self-transformation so desperately needed by the prosperous.

No doubt there had to be a national act of "generosity" before any effort could be made to dig into the real nature of poverty in a society capable of cybernetic production. By the late fall of 1965 the churches were questioning the importance of their welfare programs, and some executives of welfare projects formerly operated by the churches were wondering what the churches should do now that the government had moved in with more funds than the churches could ever assemble. Some well-known foundations also had to look around for other ways to employ their vast resources.

Church Members and Guilt

More imaginative church executives, however, were already looking forward to a new day in the mission of the church which now would be gradually relieved of its social welfare responsibilities in order to engage in its basic and eternal function—the transformation and commitment of individual and institutional life to the service of God.

Meanwhile, the day still had not arrived when church members could feel any lively personal guilt for the plight of the poor. This is desperately urgent. It would be exceedingly harmful to American life if it were discovered a generation from now that people in poverty have been kept there. This would have a traumatic reaction on the churches, for there has been obvious self-congratulation in church circles that the Economic Opportunity Act represents the fruit of numerous church consultations on and explorations of poverty.

Possible disillusionment of the nation and the churches, bad as that would be, would not be the worst effect of failure to win the war against poverty. The worst result would be that the poor will stay in poverty, unless the prosperous are converted in their attitudes. There can be no conversion of attitudes, no transformation of the hearts of the prosperous, until they have become painfully conscious of their guilt and have accepted it in all its meaning.

Jesus encountered this difficulty in Jerusalem in his ministry to the Scribes, the Pharisees and the publicans. As far as they were concerned, it was as difficult for him to justify his interest in the poor as it was for him to justify his concern for sinners. In the minds of the prosperous, who are often self-righteous, the poor and the sinners were identical, so why not lump them together? This is still being done in contemporary society.

Jesus did succeed in arousing a sense of guilt, but he did not succeed in making the prosperous, self-righteous people of his time face the guilt as being their own. Instead, they projected their guilt upon him and took him to the Cross. His innocence of their kind of guilt made it easier for them to make him a victim. He was so utterly unlike them that unity against him was easy to achieve, at least long enough to eliminate him as the source of irritation arousing their guilty feelings. There is a historic difficulty in making persons or societies deal directly with the causes of guilty feelings, and it will be no easier now than it has in the past for the prosperous to face their guilt for keeping the poor in poverty.

However, there is a new element in the present situation that makes success in this regard more likely. In the days when Jesus proclaimed the Christian mission it was utterly impossible to do away with poverty. There was simply not enough of what people needed to supply them all. The great teaching story of the feeding of the thousands sets an ideal for the ages, and we may be thankful for its fixed spot in the literature of the Church, but when it was first told as a communion story, it had to be symbolic. There was literally not enough bread for all with some left over. But the ideal is there, and if we learn someday how to share what we have, an intelligently limited population can be filled, with plenty left over. The guilt of the prosperous today is heavier than at any time in the past because now they can do something that they have never before been able to do. For the first time in history the ideal of eliminating poverty through increased production and population control is a technical possibility. This makes our failure to eliminate it a crime against God and his children.

Perhaps this should be illustrated, because it loses force when discussed in the abstract. On the day before this paragraph was written, three married couples whose lives are deeply committed to the church were together at dinner following Sunday service. They were at a vacation site owned by one of the couples, and the conversation turned to a recent incident when the house where they were dining had been broken into. The police had made an investigation and reported that some poor people in the vicinity were being watched. On hearing this, one person present took the position that these people were shiftless, untrustworthy, destructive and generally worthless. Another person said that they were impossible to help and had become that way because they enjoyed being poor, foot-loose and fancy-free. Only one person at the dinner table felt that the guilt for the housebreaking was not entirely upon the shoulders of the housebreaker but also upon the shoulders of anyone prosperous enough to have a house lived in only part of the time.

Generally speaking, he who lives in the community of the prosperous does so through influences over and beyond his control, and he who lives in the community of the impoverished may be there through factors lying beyond *his* control. What a pity that those within the two communities regard each other as enemies!

Transformation of "Self"

Perhaps we should be reminded at this point that Fingarette's studies show us that we do not secure transformation of the "self" until we come face to face with the reality of our own personal guilt and grapple with it in its full dimensions. The thief will not quit stealing as long as he can "rationalize" and say that it is not really stealing when *he* does it. In *his* case (he may say) he is only appropriating what he has really earned. Most clerks who steal from employers make this handy rationalization.

It is easier to confront a thief with *his* guilt than it is to confront the prosperous of our day with *their* guilt for keeping the poor in poverty. The law forbids stealing, and we can use fear of the law to induce emotional excitement, thus generating a temporary feeling of guilt in the thief when we catch him. There is no law against thinking of the poor in any way we choose.

We cannot walk up to prosperous people and tell them that their attitudes are wrong. This will make matters worse. We can catch a thief in the act, but we cannot "catch" an attitude, even when people make statements that expose their attitude in full light. How can we get at this? What force can ever achieve conversion of the attitudes of the prosperous?

Will the proof emerging from sociological studies, that the prosperous are guilty, be convincing enough to obtain wholesale acceptance of that guilt? The evidence is against the possibility that truth in and of itself is likely to produce significant changes. Truth is often difficult to obtain, but it is not at all difficult to ignore once it has been obtained. The general public is not greatly influenced by facts, no matter how convincing their proof.

Can we confront the prosperous with their guilt by mass communication? Can we preach the facts by TV, radio and film, and finally obtain a genuine and wholesale conversion of the public attitude? This probably would be possible, but it is unlikely that it will be attempted, because the prosperous who control the mass media are the least likely source of a sense of real guilt. They can afford to show sympathy for the poor and manifest a real concern for getting them out of their poverty. This is good business. But it is too much to expect that they will face the truth of their share in keeping people in poverty. If the mass media cannot resist the temptation of selling items that have a proved history of causing lung cancer, how can they be expected to face a less tangible sin against life? How can any prosperous person feel guilty and responsible for the poor?

chapter VII

THE CHURCH IN ITS CONVERTING ROLE

Everyone is aware of the contemporary self-criticism of the churches. It may disturb some individuals, but this great uprising within the churches is a sign of health. Not often in history has the church been healthy enough to examine its own body and its own mind. Most of the self-examination has arrived at what might be called a diagnosis that the church is suffering from institutionalism, or has become an "establishment" that fattens on the *status quo*. This would seem to be what Gibson Winter is driving at in his book, *The Suburban Captivity of the Churches*; what Peter Berger laments in *The Noise of Solemn Assemblies*; and what Harvey Cox describes in *The Secular City*.

At the risk of oversimplifying a complex matter it would seem that almost all the self-criticism of the churches could be summarized under the general proposition that the churches seem to have lost their converting role. The churches have settled down into a pattern of repose: people who belong to churches are not much different from those who do not; and the community is not affected much one way or another by the existence of the local congregation, the denominational superstructure or even councils of churches on state, national or world levels.

Obviously, the argument that the church is as dead as a dodo is full of holes. All over the world pastors are under attack for their preaching, and local congregations are being upset every Sunday morning by sermons that rock the ecclesiastical boat. The National Council of Churches is not under fire year after year for no reason at all. Every major denomination has something going that its constituency shudders to contemplate: the struggles for civil rights, economic rights, educational

78

rights, family planning rights, and the right to reconsider theological doctrines.

Let us not, however, pretend that the role of the church is
clear and that everyone understands it. Although the historical
record seems to support the proposition that it is the role of the
church to serve as a converting agency or community wherein
the individual is regularly converted and whereby the patterns
of action in the community as a whole are converted, there are
numbers of people who act as if they believe that the true role
of the church is to help people adjust in tranquility to almost
anything that happens in personal or social life. The conviction
that Christians are converted people whose main job is to convert the world has been largely supplanted by the proposition
that Christians are people who have adjusted to the world
through acquisition of a frame of mind wherein abides the
"peace that passes understanding" regardless of what one's life
is like or what is happening in society.

The idea that religion is strictly a personal affair and one's
private business is not new. The notion that the internal "experience" of God is the ultimate test of truth in religion and
of the meaning of the church has deep roots in American life.
It has already been noted that in *The Lively Experiment,* the
eminent church historian, Sidney E. Mead, has traced for us how
the American society produced an emphasis upon unrestricted
individualism in economic behavior while giving rise to the
emphasis on personal religious experience as the ultimate test for
truth in theology and the nature of the church. These two
strong currents merged to produce a society in which the church
was divorced from the state in a rigid fashion. This divorce
went so far as to convince many that the church should stay out
of activities labeled "political" and confine itself to the purely
"religious." Religion, one would be led to believe by these inter-
preters, is mainly a matter of keeping peace of mind, peace of
heart, and peace of soul intact while one continues to behave as
convenience and advantage suggest, both in personal affairs and
in social procedures. Mead concludes that we may finally achieve

religious anarchy and substitute Americanism for theology and the public school for the church.

In any case, the converting role of the church has been pushed into the background. Protestants do not wish to be charged with being anti-Catholic and therefore do not attempt to convert Catholics. Christians hesitate as to whether or not they should try to convert Jews. Either they leave them alone or hold joint services with them a few times a year. The strong reaction against emotionalism in religion gradually produced an end to revivalism and there came the birth of emphasis on Christian education. The optimistic assumption that children could be nurtured into a Christian way of life, so that they would lead lives better than those required by their parents and community influences, was a witness to the gentle hope that springs eternal: namely, that we can somehow find a way to grow up and also avoid agonized decision-making about our own lives and our social procedures.

Our distaste for being converted, or, for that matter, our distaste for trying to convert our social practices is easily understood. Life is hard enough when we discover that our favorite cake is not good for us. It is much harder when we discover that our favorte prejudice is bad not only for us but also for everybody else. It is a hellish experience to be forced to face one's guilt and then be nudged, nurtured, herded and finally cornered by some Nathan who says, "Thou art the man." When the church does this, it is being true to the converting role which is its fundamental reason for being.

What Is a Disciple?

When we come to the closing words in the Book of Matthew, the gospel of the church, we encounter the Great Commission: to go to the whole world and "make" disciples of all the nations. What is a disciple? Skip the fancy definitions. A disciple is a learner who can face the truth about himself and what he is doing. Christianity is a religion concerned with the one basic feature that sets it off and makes it superior to all other religions. This basic feature is the insistence that God loves men enough to die for them and in this way manifests the divine nature and exhibits the divine responsibility. But Christianity goes further, and this is where it splits the earth wide open. Christianity insists that *converted people* will manifest this divine nature and exhibit this divine responsibility. To be a Christian is not a matter of mere affiliation. It is the personal decision to love our brothers, whom we have not seen, in the same way that God loves us before we are born and after we are dead.

No one today is really against conversion. We just do not quite know how to do it, because revivalism doesn't work, and pastoral counseling has generally (in parish practice) misunderstood the non-directive method and made it into a non-directional influence. One might even ask to what extent the desire to be non-directive in pastoral care has produced a non-directional church. This is not to ridicule the theory of pastoral counseling based on the insights of Carl Rogers (and others). It is to raise questions about the exercise of the theory in actual practice.

It was much easier to convert frontiersmen from their lusty violence in a small community where everybody knew what everybody else was up to than it is to convert people whose open social behavior is generally accepted and whose private behavior is perfectly concealed. In short, in the frontier society it was much easier to make people feel guilty and accept personal responsibility for their guilt than it is in ours. Furthermore, the very features pointed to by Sidney Mead as lying at the root of our highly individualized religious sense also made the individual of a century ago more keenly alive to his personal damnation and his need for personal redemption.

Things are different now. God is hidden behind Mars, which is being probed by a Mariner with a staring eye. As a psychiatrist put it to me on a street corner not long ago:

"I was converted in a Methodist revival when I was fourteen and I somehow had the insight that it wouldn't last, for I went home and prayed that it would last. It was lost. Now I don't believe that there is anything to worship. We live in a universe of law, and all we need to do is study the laws and try to stay alive."

After the psychiatrist and I boarded our bus, he showed me the front page of *The New York Times*, on which appeared several items about war, mayhem and nuclear dangers. He said, "All of this depresses me so. I can hardly bring myself to read it." The question about this man is whether or not he feels any guilt about what he is and what he reads. Maybe he does, but he did not show it. If he can be brought to see his guilt, how can he be made to feel responsible? He needs self-transformation. I think he would admit that. He needs conversion, and I believe he is a good enough psychiatrist to realize that he has this need, else why did he wistfully tell me of a conversion that failed to last?

My reason for saying that he needs conversion is that he obviously feels that he is lost and the world is lost. If he cannot read the news on the front page, what must he feel about the deeper news of our world, which is not usually spread before the awareness but must be searched out with great care by one who has a deep concern?

At the outset of this chapter I said that there is good reason to believe that the uprising of self-criticism in the church is due to the church's failure to carry out its converting role. Because the church cannot at this moment convert either persons or social procedures, it is called "captive" and "irrelevant" by those who have hopes for the church—hopes brighter than its current accomplishments.

What would make it possible for the church to be converted enough to become effective in its converting role? I think that we can tackle this problem by dealing with the specific issue raised in this book. How can the prosperous be so converted in their attitudes that they will become their "brother's keeper" in the higher, more responsible, and more loving sense?

The church must bring the prosperous into immediate experience on the side of the poor. This is to say that we must do what Jesus did. He did not invite the sinners to dine with him; he went to have dinner with them. There is vast difference between asking people to come into our experience and our being ready to go into their experience. One of the favorite dogmas of Alcoholics Anonymous is that only an alcoholic can help another alcoholic. Maybe this is true. It is certain that those who understand sorrow can better help those in grief. *How can the church bring the prosperous into poverty at least far enough for them to feel guilty and face their responsibility?* I wish to suggest two steps.

Two Steps for the Church

First, the church should take the lead in getting people involved in the kinds of community organization needed by the poor in order to strive for the goals they want to reach. If the poor want to do something about their housing they must be organized. They obviously cannot organize themselves or they would not be poor. Let the church take the lead in finding the necessary funds, and let the prosperous church members get into the community organization, not as leaders but as followers and supporters. They will always be outsiders from the wrong (prosperous) part of town (a new twist!). But they will find out how guilty they are for things they never knew about before. They will take a short step toward feeling responsible, and that is when self-transformation takes place.

Meanwhile, let the church pour statistics into its own mainstream. Let it hammer home the truth about what society is like. Excite the visions of the prosperous with the tremendous potentials of social planning, and raise the hue and cry on behalf of what Kenneth Boulding calls "the post-civilization era." Post-civilization does not mean the end of human life, but it does suggest the dawn of a new era as far advanced beyond what we know today as barbarism was from the civilization now becoming obsolete.

The church's role as converting agent involves the proclamation of the New Jerusalem, which is a possibility for every succeeding generation. Our generation simply faces a greater opportunity for great good or vast evil. The increase of power is potentially *for* life if we can be converted, and on how we feel and think about the poor and our prosperity the nature of our social structure depends. Whether we perish or live as a society may depend in large measure on whether or not the churches can convert the attitudes of the prosperous, and this ultimately means whether or not the teaching and preaching of the churches can motivate enough prosperous people to join the ranks of the poor who cannot get out of poverty until their prosperous brethren are a new people.

About 70 per cent of the poor are white. This means that of the 35,000,000 citizens in poverty 28,000,000 are white. But this means also that when 7,000,000 colored people are in poverty the percentage jumps sharply to 35 per cent of our colored population. In Harlem, Philadelphia, Rochester, Chicago —as well as in the South—vast difficulties confront the prosperous Negro and the prosperous white who wish to establish firsthand experience with their brethren in poverty. Discouraging experiences are reported in efforts to get prosperous people involved as learners under the tutelage of the poor. It is difficult to do this even in the colored population, which has the advantage of the current civil rights emphasis. It is more difficult to do it with the white who are poor, for it is natural for all of us to conclude that any deserving white person should be prosperous.

The perfect way to get our change of mind would be for us to get into the predicament of the poor. We cannot do this, nor can one simply walk across town or take a subway and join the poor on one or two evenings a week. *The church must find new ways of involving the prosperous in the community of the poor if it is to carry out its role of converting the attitudes and behavior of the prosperous.*

We are hearing much about the renewal of the church. It

may come as a surprise to many that this plea for renewal has not centered around more Bible reading and private prayer nor has it put the emphasis on congregational worship. These seem to be accepted as natural fruits of renewal, if it ever comes. The call for renewal is generally in the framework of a demand that the churches get into the business of converting society. This call presumably takes for granted that much converting of individuals will be necessary if the church ever gets up enough steam to convert social procedures.

One secular magazine sees trouble ahead for the churches if they take this call to renewal with any great seriousness. The senior editor of *Look* surveyed the call for renewal in *Look's* issue of July 27, 1965, and concluded with these ominous words: "As it grows stronger, as the church surges back into the world, the turmoil that shakes Protestantism will grow more, not less, intense. We may yet find out why the prudent Romans fed their lions on Christian meat." [1]

Why would this discerning editor make this statement? Because the resistance our society will offer to any criticism of its practices will be reinforced by the neurotic sense of insecurity the United States seems to be manifesting as a world power. The persistent cry that notable movements designed to bring the one-fifth of the nation out of their poverty are either socialistic or communistic has been temporarily hushed by the Economic Opportunity Act, which is not really designed to provide basic changes in our social procedures. As it becomes more and more apparent that we will not be able to win the war against poverty without major revisions in our handling of the resources of the cybernetic revolution, we may discover that the church is the only major institution that dares raise a voice. This will mean that the church will be under fire because it will express a minority opinion—as all new opinions necessarily are.

We are now only beginning to move toward world poverty in its full horror. Gunnar Myrdal reminds us that, "In India

---

[1] T. George Harris, "The Battle of the Bible," *Look.* July 27, 1965, Vol. 29, No. 15, p. 20. Used by permission.

agricultural production for three years has not been rising appreciably, while population is increasing by 2.5 per cent, possibly more." Myrdal lists the nations where wholesale starvation would be taking place were it not for American shipments of foodstuffs. Then he comes to the problem:

"A main impediment to the utilization of the new technology capable of solving the problem is political, institutional and attitudinal. The power in many underdeveloped countries is in the hands of reactionary people who have an interest in preventing these changes in land ownership and tenancy that would increase the opportunities and incentives for the peasantry to try to improve their lot." [2]

People in the United States can easily ask why the prosperous people in India do not "wise up" before it is too late. We could ask the same questions about any part of agricultural or industrial America! It seems clear that at this point India does not have a church with the membership, the status or the existing witness to be a converting agent. Whether India is ripening for a communist "conversion" is a good question, and what goes for India also goes for all of southeast Asia and most of Africa. Latin America has a potential church for the converting role, but the churches in Latin America thus far have done about as much as anyone else to keep the poor in poverty.

Church Renewal Demand

The demand for church renewal is actually a demand that the church turn against the very things that make possible what the church has been striving for in the United States. The church has tried to become numerically strong and financially successful while placing at the same time a tremendous value on personal freedom to think and act as one pleases. Granted that this freedom to act and think as one pleases always has had certain doctrinal or behavioral limitations, they were minimum in nature and usually not diligently enforced. They were lacking

---

[2] Gunnar Myrdal, "The American Farmer in the World Economic Revolution" (an address made at the National Farmers Union Convention, Chicago, Ill. March 15, 1965).

in broad social implications. For example, the Methodists were against dancing, tobacco, alcoholic beverages and gambling. The Episcopalians were against innovations in their liturgies, and the Baptists stoutly insisted on baptism by immersion. Using their denominational differences as a base, the churches in the United States have been able to convince a huge number of people that their loyal church membership will not only "save" the American way of life but will actually make it available for the whole world. On the whole, the American churches have been more concerned with the pastoral care of their memberships than with the prophetic evaluation of the kind of society their members have been creating and supporting. The church has achieved success with its members and neglected its role as a social prophet. It is the role of the social prophet to ask what God asks of a society.

The demand for church renewal is proving to be an upsetting influence, because it has apparently moved to the point where the church is being called to take a more critical view of its own life and a much more realistic view of its environment. The very factors that have contributed to the success of the churches are now charged with being the source of their lacks. Denominationalism, which permitted vast freedom in the choices one could make in religious affiliation, is being blasted right and left. The proud claim that each individual can be depended upon to find and know the truth about God and the Bible is challenged by the new demands of scholarship which insist that theology and the Bible require serious study and offer rewards only to those who will put forth great effort. Even more upsetting is the emergence of the new technology, better known as the cybernetic revolution. This gigantic eruption into human history of the computer linked to the machine is throwing the whole world into turmoil. We now see brought out into the open every latent conflict, whether racial, national, sectional, social or ideological.

The emerging call for the church to take up its social role as a converting agent invites the church to change the people who now compose it and also to change the social patterns that have brought the church to its present flower. This partly explains the rising internal conflict within the church, a conflict which no doubt will increase in intensity and continue to produce tremendous anxiety in clergy and laity alike.

At no point is the need for conversion of personal attitudes and social procedures more clearly illuminated than in connection with the problems of the poor kept in poverty by the attitudes of the prosperous. The handiest illustration of this is the conflict over Medicare. The predicament of the aged and the aging is terrible and is growing worse as people are kept alive longer and living costs increase year by year. At least 6½ millions of people past the age of 65 live on a total annual income of $1,000 or less. These people simply cannot meet the costs of illness in any form because they cannot meet the costs of living in health. I have participated in many a discussion in which church people have argued that no person in this country needs go without adequate medical and hospital care. Even when these people were told that they had fellow church members who had been required to swear that they were in poverty in order to get welfare assistance, they were unconvinced. They simply could not believe that some people would suffer illness unattended before taking the pauper's oath. Some of them said that they would not hesitate to take the pauper's oath if that was required in order to get needed help in time of sickness, but one wonders if this would be as easy for them as they seemed to think.

We cannot take the space to describe all the areas of our contemporary personal and social need where changes cannot come until there have been radical conversions of mind and heart. Every effort leading to conversion will involve the church in controversy within its own body and with its surrounding society of habits, procedures, laws and moral consents.

In short, the church will be deeply involved in controversy if it takes up its converting role. The controversy in which it will be engaged at this point in its history will not be as simple in its contrasts as in the "good old days" when the church could stand forthrightly against prostitution, drunkenness and high-stake gambling. The new forms of prostituting human life are more subtle and have too much social approval to give the church a lily-white position. Forms of intoxication now include more than alcoholic indulgence. They include luxury, position, power and social status. Kinds of gambling are more numerous and operate under the form of commercial enterprises with the control of the "game" generally in the hands of the prosperous and the victims at the "table" the poor in poverty.

Whether the church itself can be converted in time to fulfill its role as an agent of conversion in the emerging post-civilization is a real issue. Perhaps there has never been a generation for whom the Parable of the New Wine and the Old Wineskins has been more forceful. It is the role of the church to convert the contemporary mind and the contemporary social procedures to accommodate the vastness of God's Spirit pouring in upon the world—pouring in with the form of cybernetic threat and promised blessing. Whether we will be converted or not is a matter of life and death. This casts the role of the church in its eternal setting, for the church is the door to either life or death —even for the church itself.

chapter VIII

THE INDIVIDUAL CHRISTIAN AND SOCIAL STAGNATION

An interesting event in history is the fall of a nation. Old Testament writers took note of the fallen Babylon with some relish, but they also did their best to remind the people of Israel that what happened to others could happen also to them. Gibbon was so curious about the rise and decline of the Roman Empire that he spent a good portion of his lifetime writing about it, seeking an explanation for the fall of that vast enterprise which still strikes us with its daring and organizational excellence.

In the past several years Arnold Toynbee, a remarkable historian with an unusual humility in spite of vast learning, has been trying to put into a workable theory an explanation of the rise and fall of whole civilizations. Toynbee resists the temptation to take refuge in mystical explanation. He is after explanations that have roots in human behavior. He wants to know what people and their leaders do to cause the downfall of the very civilization they work so hard to create.

In general, it appears that success in reaching social goals may tend to make a society stagnant, and it will then suffer decline because it is not responsive to what Toynbee calls a "new challenge." Because the successful society has become accustomed to doing things in certain ways, it begins to think that these ways are the only ones needed, and will tend to resist any emerging demands because they call for new ways of doing things.

Stagnation can be the main social feature of a primitive tribe in some out-of-the-way part of the world. Once the tribe has hit upon rituals, practices and rules governing tribal behaviors it will put a high value on them and may even bestow on them religious origins, which makes it more difficult to change them even in a minor way. Sophisticated societies tend to do the same. In Adam Smith's historic treatment of how the marketing and manufacturing of goods operates, he sees in the absolutely free market of unrestrained competition a mysterious law of the universe which somehow forces that kind of market automatically to produce just prices, fair wages and the best possible quality. Smith's *Wealth of Nations* is deeply involved in notions that are not only economic but also theological. Our concern is limited to the way that Smith's viewpoints tended first to stabilize and then to hold in a somewhat stagnant pattern the economic transactions of the Western world. The Great Depression of the 1930's was preceded by almost a century of deep conviction that the marketplace would automatically take care of wages, prices and quality of goods if it were left unhindered by laws, regulations and fiscal or monetary controls. Prosperity was "just around the corner" if nothing was done to change what was being practiced. A long period of stagnation in economic theory and practice nearly wrecked the social and economic system of the Western world.

Long periods of success in social movements produce deep convictions that the formula has at last been found for eternal success. Success in social movements usually is measured in terms of goals dealing with some kind of expansion. After the Civil War the nation was growing westward, it was building railroads, and new cities appeared on the plains. In spite of periodic setbacks the procedures that people had come to believe in for business, education, religion and expansion seemed to work. This was rapidly becoming "the American way" of doing things, and as long as goals were set in terms of more and more expansion of almost everything, the people were happy and could endure harsh setbacks because they were sure that they were only minor intrusions in the main stream of a manifest destiny. The Great Depression shook the confidence of the nation and undermined faith in its long-established processes. Furthermore, the goals which had provided such strong motivation lost their gleam for most citizens. The drive for expansion slacked off, and young people became more interested in the size of the pension than in the size of the distant goal.

Every society tries to find ways of making things work well enough for the accomplishment of social goals. Ordinarily, the goals are hazy in the minds of most citizens and are not always clear to political and other leaders. The national goals of the United States at this point in history are probably more specific than they have been since the beginning of the nation, but even now they are loosely defined in terms of civil rights for all, jobs for those able to work, freedom to develop one's highest potential, and the like.

It is probably good for a society to have a loose definition of goals, because goals have a way of being contradictory. For example, a society with a goal of freedom for all its citizens will immediately encounter the problem of limiting *my* use of freedom so that it will not prevent *your* use of freedom. Thus the goal of freedom for all must have the contradictory goal of limited freedom for all.

Characteristics of Society

Having said this about the haziness of goals and their contradictory nature, we still must recognize that any society is characterized by the way its citizens have generalized their consents into a workable pattern of agreement. This consensus alone permits a government to succeed in such operations as the power to tax, to engage in international affairs and to impose authority with force upon all citizens. The United States represents an amazing society with increasing uneasiness about its role and goals in the world of nations. It is a nation held together by its systems of common expectations. These are rooted in religion, cultural habits and political convictions. Added to these common expectations is a long history of economic expansion which now reaches for the moon and beyond with the emergence of the cybernetic revolution. It is under the impact of the cybernetic revolution that the United States suddenly finds itself lofted into a position as world leader. In short, the United States has become a successful nation, and there are signs that it will do what other nations have done when they have become successful: they have become stagnant.

When a primitive tribe settles down to its fixed pattern of mythologies, rituals and social practices, it translates them usually into a religiously sanctioned social process simply because the tribe's affairs have become stabilized enough for the tribe to reach more or less desired goals. We recognize this immediately as a stagnant society.

When we who live in the United States settle down to a fixed pattern of response to our continuing problems we have the normal problem of recognizing our mythologies, rituals and religiously-sanctioned practices for what they really are. The tribesman looks at his stagnant society and wonders why it falters in the new situation. He cannot see why it fails to work now because it worked so well for his fathers. In like manner the citizen of the United States may not recognize the stagnant nature of his society which continues to use the same old methods for meeting new problems.

For example, consider the necessity of having houses for people to live in. The system we use for providing houses for citizens in this country is not the same system used by the Danes, the Dutch or the Yugoslavs. This is not to say that they use the same system or that their systems are better or worse than ours. It is only to say that our systems of providing housing are not the only ones in the world, and they may or may not be the best for our citizens. Some of our methods worked very well in the days of agricultural expansion, but the question now is whether they work in a period of urban concentration. Efforts to change the pattern of providing houses in which people can found and develop home life are frustrated by the strongly structured patterns that now exist, but it is very clear that these patterns will not provide the housing we will need for the generation already entering our elementary schools. The present housing pattern will probably take care of the prosperous but on a gradually declining plane of satisfaction. The poor as well as all lower-income groups will be left out in the cold as usual, and nothing short of a major revolution in the building trades unions, methods of construction and methods of finance will meet the needs of the coming generation. Our society is socially stagnant when it comes to the provision of housing for our people.

Without going into great detail we should note other areas of our society where social stagnation threatens our welfare as a nation. In every instance this social stagnation serves the interests of the important segment of the population that lives in prosperity. This stagnant feature works to the detriment of the poor. As we have noted, the stagnant patterns of our housing procedures work with some degree (although the degree seems to get smaller and smaller) to the satisfaction of the prosperous while working against the poor who cannot get out of poverty as long as they are required to dwell in slums, both rural and urban.

Consider how stagnant our educational procedures have been and continue to be. It is still largely assumed that every family should be able to pay the costs of higher education for its youth, although the cost of elementary and high school education has long been a responsibility of the whole society. Major breakthroughs in this area do not appear on the horizon because the prosperous hold the power to make decisions, and tax support for higher education of all who can qualify would mean an increase in taxes. Furthermore, the mythology that anyone who wants a college education can get one continues to prevail on the grounds that: "If I worked *my* way through college, anybody can." This is to say that: "What was good for me is good now for everybody else." The fly in the ointment is the vast increase in educational costs in the last few years, and there are more increases to come. There are probably fewer self-help jobs today in comparison to the larger numbers enrolled in our colleges. It is harder than it used to be to work one's way through college.

We are socially stagnant when it comes to getting much of the necessary work done in our society. Reference has already been made to the untouched jobs of our city streets, waterfronts, parks, playgrounds and forests. We may ask also why there are not thousands of jobs for necessary work in the graphic and performing arts. When the New York Philharmonic was subsidized in the summer of 1965 to give free concerts in Central Park, more than 70,000 people came to the first one. When will we decide that our great cities will have music as well as airports, and musicians in addition to policemen?

Societies become stagnant when procedures settle down and objectives remain fixed. A society becomes stagnant when it reaches the end of what it set out to do. This is the point at which its life is threatened. Success is often more dangerous than failure. So successful was the dinosaur in becoming big that it finally became too big to survive. It ate too much and moved too slowly, but it did succeed in becoming big.

The American society cannot be discussed as if it exists alone in the world. When England moves, the United States is affected; when England refuses to move, this also has an effect upon us. Poverty in our country is related to poverty in Mexico.

The stagnation of any national society is a threat to the welfare of the world, because the world moves more and more as a social fabric of one great cloth, with different patterns here and there.

This means that the Christian churches in the United States have a major opportunity in promoting the welfare of the people of the world through winning the war against poverty, but this war cannot be won without appropriate measures being taken to get out of our present social stagnation and permit the development of new forms.

We have indicated already a few symptoms of current stagnation by referring to housing, education and limiting concepts about the kinds of work necessary for our social welfare. Now let us ask a personal question.

Duties of Individual Christians

How can the individual Christian do anything about these problems so complex that the Congress of the United States is often thwarted in its efforts to reach decisions leading to appropriate lines of action?

Individual Christians who have become sensitive to their own role in the world really want to be their brother's keeper in the higher sense. They wish to be keepers of the poor in such a way that the poor are brought out of poverty. But what can one person do? This nagging question must have valid answers. Let us face the question as honestly as possible.

The individual Christian cannot do much in isolated action because the individual in our society is relatively powerless. This is a distinctive feature of an urban culture. One of the reasons for the continued success of the television drama with a lone gunman carrying his weapon on his hip is the splendor of an individual making good without aid. We like the idea of St. George tackling the Dragon, and once in a while we get a glimpse of some individual standing alone for a great and noble cause, but gradually the great orator, the great statesman and the great reformer have been supplanted by the careful organizer and the patient planner unseen within the structure of a group.

Having said all this, we realize that one great fact remains, and the individual Christian should make it part of his theology. *God apparently has made us in such a way that each person is the center of a sphere of opportunity, and in his particular sphere there are openings for his individual initiative.*

This is a tremendously important element of Christian belief. If Jesus of Nazareth had not seen his life as being within a sphere of opportunity he would not have discovered the openings waiting for his initiative. The individual Christian must follow Jesus in this respect. Each of us is limited by the sphere in which we are the center, but we are also given the openings for initiative in that sphere. These are not openings to any other living person. Two men living side by side in the same town may dwell in *similar* spheres but they are not *identical* by any means, nor are their openings for initiative the same.

A Christian businessman who works in a grocery store may not find the same openings for initiative as do a farmer or a teacher. A doctor may find one differing from that of a lawyer. It is fairly certain that any Christian individual who decides to answer the call to become a valid keeper of the poor will find ways to help get the poor out of poverty. It is also likely that only a good Christian will take the offered opportunity. Recently I talked to a lifelong friend, a physician, who told me that he had formally refused to give medical treatment to young men in a nearby Job Corps camp if it meant going to the camp, because treatment would have to be at a reduced fee, and besides, he asked, "How many hoodlums will be there?" This physician had not taken into consideration his power to seize this opening for his personal initiative to help win the war against poverty. He did not realize that his sphere of influence was so powerful and that no one else was at the center of his particular sphere. What he decided *not* to do as an individual will be left undone.

Let us not be too hard on this physician who had never before refused to treat patients because they lacked money. He did not want to seize the opportunity, and in this he is not alone. As a whole, the community where he resides is not too keen about a Job Corps camp with more than 200 boys moving in as a result of federal action against poverty. These 200 young men provide opportunities for individual Christians of the community to take initiatives of various kinds, but the taking of these openings requires much more than good intentions. It requires judgment of what is appropriate, tact, tenacity and a maximum faith in human potential.

The poor live all across the land, but the eyes of many of their fellow Americans are dull and cannot see the poor as persons who can be helped. They are seen as problems too complex to solve or as nuisances to cope with by various defenses.

The individual Christian with wit and spirit enough to seize the openings of initiative available to him in the war against poverty is rare. The poor are not easy to see as people who can be helped. Christians generally have the wrong attitudes toward the poor, and one thing the individual Christian can do is shape up his own attitudes and seize all possible opportunities. With 35,000,000 of our citizens in poverty, the nearest opportunity is not far away.

The second step the individual Christian can take is to face up to the fact that he may not have the skills necessary to take the opportunities of initiative, and therefore no amount of urging on grounds of Christian obligation will force him to do it. Individuals usually will not do what they are not prepared to do, and the average Christian knows that he is by no means prepared to take the nearest opportunity to identify his life with a poor person. If he is not actually afraid of the poor person, he probably is suspicious and thinks that the person is in poverty for some hidden but justifiable reasons. In some other way the individual Christian may avoid the available opportunity to help the poor. He is unwilling to admit that he does not know how to help, and will therefore invent other reasons to cover up his awareness of his inability.

One function of any institution is the enrichment of the life of the individual. Jesus formed the "institution" of the group of disciples very early in his ministry, and was acknowledging his individual need in doing so. He had been for a time one of the followers of John the Baptist and knew the values of belonging to a group. With the disciples Jesus had a training situation, and much of his teaching was for their preparation to do a clearly-defined task. The New Testament contains some early-church manuals of instruction for the first Christians.

Congregational Duties

Each local congregation is supposed to be a training school for Christian obedience and Christian service. Congregational worship is the regular celebration of the whole membership gathered to worship the Divine Presence, but the attention of the congregation should also be directed to the special skills that must be developed if the individual Christian is to be an obedient Christian. In the language of this chapter and within the confines of this book, the congregation exists to help the individual Christian recognize and move into the opportunities that may open for helping the poor out of poverty.

On the practical level this means that the local congregation would first take a look at its own membership. Most congregations have a few poverty-stricken members. These really do not belong to the community of the impoverished but generally are people who once had enough to live on but now lack the means of a decent existence. In my own ministry I found a woman from an old established family in the church. Everyone thought that she had enough to support her, but I discovered that she was living on a budget of $8 per month for food. This alerted me to the possibility of a larger problem, and by careful pastoral searching I found a number of other persons in similar need. The average affluent congregation has a number of extremely needy members who for reasons of pride go without proper food and medical care. Real tact is required to be helpful in these cases, but no congregation dares neglect these persons who are not counted among the 35,000,000 in poverty.

When the congregation has looked into its own membership, it then helps the individual by forming a group of individuals into what is currently being called a "task force"—the same old committee by another name. Committees are very useful when they have a definite task to perform and an important body to which they report. This Anti-Poverty Task Force in the local church will then move out to make visible that which everybody knows by now is invisible. This may sound simple, but one of the best steps prosperous Christians in many a town and city could take is to walk through the poverty-stricken part of town or along a poverty row in the country. People in New York, Chicago and all the nation's Middletowns are like cows in a pasture: they follow the same old trails day after day and finally come to the conclusion that they know what the city is like. A Sunday afternoon walk for the prosperous of Philadelphia or Rochester along the streets of poverty in those cities might have spared them rioting in 1964. In the summer of 1965 there probably would not have been nearly 200 million dollars' worth of property damage and terrible loss of life in the Watts section of Los Angeles if prosperous Christians had previously had a firsthand look at and a firsthand smell of poverty. The Congress of the United States would do well to walk the streets of Washington, D. C., but the churches there might do it first.

These cities are no worse than others. They serve as handy illustrations and are mentioned because rioting within them had strong overtones of economic repression as well as denial of civil rights. But poverty was at the root, and who knows what will happen if poverty-stricken white people are ever inflamed to revolt against their plight? Any local congregation in the United States would be a more Christian congregation after following a congregational plan for small groups to walk along the streets where the poor dwell. This would be a preliminary step toward training the individual Christian in knowing how to help the poor. At least we can begin by looking at the outside of the house.

The local congregation may then be ready to meet with the poor on grounds that are familiar to the poor. In New York City the *Metropolitan Urban Service Training* project sponsored by the National Division of the Methodist Board of Missions and supported with enthusiasm by the Woman's Division is designed to train both clergy and laity in urban work. A major point of emphasis is on the manner of meeting with people who feel that they have no stake in a world taken for granted by the prosperous. Experience seems to bear out the assumption that people in poverty will not leave their world just to sit a while in the company of the prosperous. The prosperous individual must know how to leave his world and at least show readiness to understand his limitations when trying to help the poor cope with poverty.

Each local congregation will have to be led by the Holy Spirit in finding its way, but training prosperous Christians to meet their 35,000,000 brothers and sisters in poverty is a major obligation. This is a new element in the emerging mission of the Christian church in the United States. The vast mission fields in this country offer a greater obligation than the American church has faced. Not only do we lack clergy in sufficient numbers for the leadership task, but many of those we have must be retrained for new kinds of work. Not only do we lack proper buildings to carry out the church's task, but The Methodist Church is building only one and one-half churches a day when it should build at least three per day to keep pace with the population increase. Thousands of our churches are in such bad repair that they cannot pass minimum standards for housing programs involving children and youth. In community after community school facilities are so much more attractive than churches that the rising generation cannot but write the church off as a passing institution. Stagnation is the result of success, and it is now the task of the individual Christian to arouse the local congregation to what was assigned us in our charter when Jesus proclaimed "Good news for the poor!" Hardly anything offers our churches a greater opportunity than desperate human need, and all around the land the poor *exist* but do not *live*. They need the help of trained Christians.

What a change can come over a local church if individual Christians begin to see the congregation as a training center for action! The building takes on new meaning and is really worth whatever it costs to make it adequate. The study courses offered in the church catalogs and described in church periodicals are not seen as weary assignments but as the means to new social techniques that will save the nation from its illness.

Duties of Institutions

It has been stated in this book that an institution has two functions, and we have been discussing one of these as it pertains to the church. We have said that the first function is to enrich the life of the individual, and in the case of the Christian Church this enrichment is found in the training of people to possess skills for carrying out a discipleship in lively obedience to God.

The second function of an institution is to amplify the limited power of the individual into a social force directly in ratio to the skill by means of which the institution itself is led and managed. In short, the individual in our society is almost helpless in dealing with the institutions of society unless he is related to an effective institution which permits him to engage in action through it.

No individual in our society can deal effectively with the Federal Reserve System. It is an institution, dealing with other banking institutions. The individual deals with it only indirectly. A better example is the way in which contracts are written when a labor union deals with a big corporation in collective bargaining. The individual is in the contract when it is finally signed, but he did not negotiate it himself. In collective bargaining, the individual in management as well as the individual in labor is represented by an institution.

In much the same way the individual Christian finds that the institutional church exists on at least three levels. He knows it most intimately on the local level, but he usually is aware that the local church is part of a denomination. Sometimes the denomination to which he belongs speaks on an issue, and he may or may not agree with what his denomination says, but he will at least admit that an issue has been addressed on a level and with a force he could not command as an individual. If the denominational level can be thought of as the second level, the third level is the interdenominational. The National Council of the Churches of Christ in the United States is an institution composed of institutional representation, and when it speaks, it speaks only for itself, but here again it speaks with a force that gives a different dimension to the individual.

It is in this manner that the individual gives existence to

institutions on various levels. Institutions speak to other institutions on related levels in society. Complications develop when this speaking takes place, because the millions of individuals who constitute the various institutions do not see eye-to-eye, and obviously what is spoken by the institution is likely to have a minority in disagreement almost every time. If it speaks and every single soul in the ranks is satisfied, one can be sure that it was not necessary or important that the institution speak at all.

It is important to observe that when social stagnation exists it prevents or inhibits speaking by individuals, denominations or groups of denominations. The stagnant situation would not exist if it failed to please a majority, and the individual Christian should be prayerfully alert to the possibility that when his denomination speaks in a way that disturbs him he may be wrong, and the denomination may be right! This would never occur to some individuals who protest denominational utterances and statements of the National Council of Churches, but it is a worthwhile thought and has from time to time applied to this writer.

One of the great contributions the individual Christian makes to his world is to help make an institution, the Holy Church, so sensitive to the needs of the world that it will not permit society to become stagnant. The early Christians stirred things up, and while it was too late to save the Roman Empire it was still early enough to start the Western world off in a new direction. Now a new era is being born, and the United States is in the center of the earth's vast, swirling, cybernetic revolution. What happens to the poor in this country in the next ten years will determine in large measure what happens to the United States and its position of world leadership.

At the center of his own sphere of initiative, the individual Christian is offered openings for individual initiative in the war against poverty. Furthermore, each Christian individual has a church which is at once a training ground for local Christian action and an institutional voice with force to deal with the great institutions of society.

At the base of the whole structure is the individual. What he does in his sphere of opportunity in seizing openings for initiative will determine, in the end, whether together we do God's will for the poor or not. Whether we stagnate and die as a society will depend on whether or not we produce individual Christians obedient to God in the sphere of which each is the center, and within which there are surprising openings for individual initiative.

chapter IX

THE POOR WHO CROWD THE GLOBE

In 1952 an important book appeared under the title, *The Geography of Hunger*. Its author was the distinguished chairman (at that time) of the United Nations Food and Agricultural Organization, Josue de Castro. The foreword was written by a Nobel Prize winner, Lord Boyd-Orr, who, with obvious caution, hinted at the possibility of a world population of three to four billion in the lifetime of his children. That was thirteen years ago, and the world population is already three and one-half billion and growing faster than ever. Poverty is spreading as fast as the population grows, and the ratio of two persons in poverty to one person in relative prosperity is the same today as it was a generation or even longer ago. It is predicted that in 2000 A.D., just 34 years from now, 80 per cent of the world's population of 4.6 billion will live in what are now undeveloped areas.

The cautious prediction of Lord Boyd-Orr that people will crowd the globe is just one more proof that even the experts have not been able to grasp fully the enormity of our world population increase. Visitors at the New York World's Fair casually glanced at the big scoreboard with its moving lights reporting our nation's growth, but its full impact reached hardly any of them.

Well-informed citizens are not so casual. "It will take all the ingenuity and energy we can muster to stave off disaster through the remaining years of this century," Thomas Ware, Chairman of International Minerals and Chemical Corporation, told the Senate Foreign Relations Committee in May, 1965. In Ware's testimony he pointed out that only 3.5 per cent of the globe's surface is arable land. He suggested the probability that in the next thirty-five years the world population will double.

Meanwhile, food production encounters one failure after another, and the poor spread over the globe.

Writing in *Science,* Dael Wolfle says:

"The time has come for an extensive systems analysis of the problems of saving planet Earth as a pleasant, productive home for mankind. . . . The fundamental problem is people. Whatever we do to increase food supplies, conserve water, improve land management or curb pollution merely postpones for a few years the day of catastrophe unless we stop increasing the number of hungry mouths." [1]

The more spectacular the prediction about population increase, the less it seems to arouse our interest. I recall a group discussion on the subject when evidence was introduced to the effect that in a certain number of years the weight of the people could equal the weight of the globe—which means that people would have devoured the globe, salt water and molten center alike! The group almost went to sleep on that one. It was just too far out to cope with.

There is probably a certain amount of good sense in not becoming too excited about the possibility that the human animal will devour the earth in much the same way that maggots consume a chunk of meat and then perish for lack of food. The human race has exhibited a peculiar streak of practical wisdom that accounts for its survival. In the long run the population problem will likely be solved.

The trouble is that Christian ethics deals with the short run as well as the long run. Christians do not pass by a person in pain with serene faith that because the person will at his death be with God, the long-run benefits for him will permit us to pass by in the immediate situation. In the long run the human race may solve the problem of poverty in the same way that it has solved some other social problems, but up to this point in human evolution the solutions achieved in the long run have been produced by people dealing with immediate situations.

[1] "Save the World," Dael Wolfle, *Science,* Vol. 149, No. 3686, p. 819, 20 August 1965. Used by permission.

This is to say that the human race will probably survive the threat of extinction through overpopulation, but if it does survive, it will be because enough people take the threat seriously to do everything possible to put into operation the lines of action that will make survival possible.

World poverty is a complex matter, and there is danger in trying to oversimplify it. On the other hand, we cannot engage in lines of action until we state them in simple terms. Usually we discover that our lines of action need to be shifted after we are on the road to our objective, and Christians should certainly take for granted that strategy in church mission will shift from time to time.

Poverty-Population Law

Let us risk a generalization about world poverty that links it to the problem of world population. This generalization is based on what seems to be solid statistical data. Let us say that it is a law of poverty and population increase. Here is the law: *The birth rate is highest among the poor and lowest among the prosperous.*

Taking it in its global aspects, we see the globe with 3½ billion people beginning to crowd its presently habitable areas. Of this vast population at least 2 billion are hungry. It is claimed that where poverty abounds fertility is increased, and the birth rate rises. We have referred to this phenomenon as a "law of poverty and population increase," but it should not be understood as being as unchangeable as the function of gravity. What we are saying is that so far this is the way things are.

What does this mean? It means that poverty in India is steadily growing worse, and at this time efforts to change the situation are not adequate. Japan has reduced its birth rate, and already there are signs that this will alleviate some of its poverty. Japan has moved so rapidly into high industrial gains that it is unclear as to whether the reduced birth rate is a result of bet-

ter economic conditions or the product of organized efforts
of the government to limit population increase through birth
control measures and the legalization of abortion.

India is not the only country where poverty is increasing,
nor is Japan the only country coming to grips with poverty
as a factor in over population. Generally, the Latin American
countries have shown increases in population, with correspond-
ing spread of poverty, while West Germany, the Netherlands,
the Scandinavian countries, England and a few other nations
have shown remarkable progress in the elimination of poverty
and the stabilization of population increase.

It is almost useless to try to make real to the average American Christian the nature of the degree of poverty on this earth.
Human life crowds the globe, and the two-thirds of God's
children who live in hunger, filth, despair and wretchedness did
not ask to be born, which fact they probably think about. They
are completely aware that they are in poverty and cannot
emerge, because the prosperous community holds the key to
the portal through which they must come out.

The problem may be different in the United States from that
in other nations. Prosperous people in some parts of the world
are more openly indifferent to what they should do to help the
poor. The rich prince or the agricultural lord of some Asian
valley is visible to other humans. Local power is thus obvious to
the poor, who know that they are being kept in "their place"
by attitudes with which they cannot or dare not cope.

A few months ago we spent several days with two wealthy
and powerful farmers from Pakistan who were visiting in this
country to study agricultural methods. They were delightful
companions and spoke excellent English. They were most dutiful
in their religious observances at dawn, for they are Moslems.
We gave them each a compass so that their faces could always
be turned eactly east at the time of prayer. We value them as
good and pleasant friends. Their view of their rights and responsibilities in relationship to the people under their charge (and
there are many) is simple. It is the view of the king or prince

toward a serf who is a serf for keeps, now and forevermore. I have found the same attitude in industry, farming and church administration in this country. When this attitude is established in connection with gaining a livelihood it may have a different face in Pakistan, India or Brazil, but it is the same problem we encounter in the United States.

A Third Proposition

Mentioning the problem in other countries exposes another problem we cannot escape dealing with if the human race is to survive.

If we consider that the birth rate is highest among the poor and lowest among the prosperous, in conjunction with the argument that the poor are kept in poverty by the attitudes of the prosperous, we come up with a third proposition: *The people in poverty will increase in numbers in any society until they constitute an overwhelming social force that will make continuation of established social procedures impossible.* In short, they will upset the prosperous and their controls by disrupting the social procedures the prosperous have found advantageous.

There is nothing new about this proposition. The poor have been storming the bastions of the rich time out of mind, and while the leaders of revolutions have not always emerged from the peasant class they have found necessary recruits there. In revolutionary situations there are more poor people than rich ones, and the poor have passionate reasons for desiring social changes.

What is new in our time is the nature of industrialization in the emerging nations and the rapid advance into the cybernetic era of the developed nations. Let us consider what industrialization means to an emerging nation. No matter where the nation is located, the development of industry requires manpower, which means that people will leave the farms because new industry cannot be developed without them. This means that industry will offer better wages to lure people from food production. In poor nations where food production is already lagging behind population increase, this probably means more food shortages or even starvation, unless the developed nations can grow and export greater food supplies to exchange for the new nation's new industrial goods.

Few of the developed nations can actually afford great export of foods and fibers at this time. Russia apparently is having vastly more trouble developing agriculture than industry. It takes longer to become a good farmer than it does to become a good engineer, and farming attracts fewer of the best workers because it offers less economic rewards in most countries. The United States has restricted its agriculture and does not have great quantities of surplus food today. Canada can export wheat and some beef, but what is all of Canada's production compared to the hunger of India alone?

The experts have been telling us for decades that we face global hunger. What no one has seen until recently is that the poor are crowding the globe and their rising demand for the fruits of technology will force the development of industry all over the earth. At the same time the flight from agriculture to industry may reduce their food production and create a world food shortage such as the human race has never seen. This process is now visible in India, and efforts are being made to resist the trend. The notion that industrialization of the emerging nations is the single solution to world poverty and global hunger is ridiculous. Unless the production of food is brought quickly to its highest capacity in every nation of the world the industrialization of nations will create more poverty, because poverty can be measured by a basic yardstick—HUNGER.

Only prosperous people can head off the disaster of global hunger. When the entire case is presented to us, it seems likely that the decision for the whole world will be made, for better or for worse, by the people of the United States.

It is assumed here that a global program for feeding the hungry would have to be launched by the United States. The decision to do this would have to include the feeding of people in communist-led or communist-dominated nations because a vast portion of the hungry population of the world is in those countries. In an earlier chapter, reference was made to Gunnar Myrdal's proposal that American agriculture should now be brought into its fullest possible production. Myrdal made this proposal in the spring of 1965. He has been telling us for several years that the greatest danger we face is our tendency to drift along. In 1956 this eminent scholar wrote:

"And then I get the feeling—and sense the anxiety—that the world is drifting towards a destiny it has not charted in advance and for which it has not been deliberately steering its course. . . . This is how crises and war come about. . . . Something is under way that at one stage, if it had been analyzed squarely and faced courageously, could have been stopped by relatively minor sacrifices, intelligently applied, but at a later date cannot be stopped at all, even by very much bigger sacrifices." [2]

Global Hunger

Global hunger is both the result of poverty and a sustaining cause of it. The end of global hunger will require definite decisions made in time. These decisions will include one to expand American agriculture instead of restricting it. This is an American decision, but it cannot be made until other nations decide to let us export food. If the export of our wheat, for example, wrecks the economy of some other nation that depends upon the export of wheat to sustain its total economy, we are not accomplishing much for the total good. This applies to every export designed to help. Christian ethics in international affairs finally comes to the question of international finance and exchange.

When we examine the full meaning of world hunger, we realize that the major issue is not that of being merciful to others for their sake. The issue is whether or not we have

---

[2] Gunnar Myrdal, *An International Economy* (New York: Harper & Brothers, 1956), p. 300. Used by permission.

enough self-interest to make the hard choices that lead to survival of the human race. If the American people decide that they want their government to launch a "Food for the Hungry" movement in the world they will have to support revisions in our way of doing business. Are we ready to help feed the people of Rumania, Poland, Czechoslovakia and Yugoslavia, as well as our once-upon-a-time friends in Cuba, China, Indonesia and several other places? The facts indicate that we are not ready and willing. Longshoremen presently will not load ships loaded with food bound from United States ports for these countries, even if the American people wanted them to do so.

Appropriations for American aid to other nations are being reduced each year although military spending for overseas operations is increasing as the United States assumes the responsibility of acting as an international policeman. Without abdicating the role of policeman, is it possible for the American people to take more active leadership in the task of feeding the hungry? Whether or not this is possible depends upon whether or not we want to do it when we discover what it means. It means active brotherhood, and there may not be in the United States that much feeling for brotherhood. The dominant feeling of the American people is one of sullen dismay that people of other nations do not seem to appreciate our tremendous efforts up to the present point. Out of this dismay is growing an evil crop of anti-foreign-aid attitudes, which in turn feed upon the fear of communism.

The climate of opinion in the United States is not favorable for a lifesaving decision on the part of the President and the Congress to move into leadership in a "Food for the Hungry" campaign on a global basis. Here again is illumination of the contemporary mind which thinks that poverty is proof that the individual or the nation of the poor is indecent, lazy, shiftless, lacking in motivation and unintelligent.

Pope John XXIII raised this question in a sharply-pointed, now famous encyclical called *Pacem in Terris* (Peace on Earth). The encyclical was deemed of sufficient importance to justify an international convocation in New York City in February, 1965. More than 2000 scholars, statesmen, clergy and others gathered. The Nobel Prize winner, Linus Pauling, said in his address:

"Our system of morality as expressed in the operating legal, social and economic structures is full of imperfections, and these imperfections have been accentuated during recent decades. There is great misery caused by the abject poverty of about half of the world's people; yet most of the scientists and technologists of the world today are working to make the rich richer and the poor poorer, or we are working on the develpment and fabrication of terrible engines of mass destruction and death whose use might end our civilization and exterminate the human race. . . . I believe that it is a violation of the natural law for half of the people of the world to live in misery, in abject poverty, without hope for the future, while the affluent nations spend on militarism a sum of money equal to the entire income of this miserable half of the world's people." [3]

In the discussions that took place in the convocation mentioned above, the points raised by the remarks of Pauling and the Papal Encyclical generally found the participants agreed on basic principles. A good example is that of a Soviet scientist speaking immediately after a Latin American economist had agreed with a French sociologist. All of them were dealing with the question of how development of anything takes place and in particular how development takes place in a country attempting to get its people out of poverty. All three speakers agreed that the poor must have help from the outside *but the help from the outside must be deeply identified and wholeheartedly involved with those being helped.* This really means that the outside help must come with no strings attached, and must remain with a willingness to rise or fall with the choices and the lines of action chosen by the people who are trying to help themselves. It is to be regretted that this important meet-

[3] Center for the Study of Democratic Institutions, The Fund for the Republic, Inc., Box 4068, Santa Barbara, California 93103, p. 3, Used by permission.

ing did not face the issue of a necessary population limitation.

This speaks to us about the mission of the church not only in lands across the sea but also in our own land. When we try to help other people improve their lives, we are in the hardest work in the world because everybody knows that it is easier to tie a child's shoes than it is to teach the child to tie his own. Real self-discipline is required to keep hands off when other hands need to learn. This is hard enough in our own land where the pressures of surrounding culture influence choices and lines of action. In other lands it is harder because some of the choices and lines of action seem too strange to work. All this means that we cannot help people get out of poverty if all we want is to have them be as we are and do as we do. Other nations may not want our social system or our economic practices, but we had better help them get out of poverty *their* way if we want them to slow down their population growth and thus reduce the rate of advance toward global tragedy.

What this means in practical terms for Christians in the United States has to be stated in political terms because our relationships with other nations are mostly political. While this is being written, Vietnam is bleeding, and Southeast Asia is threatening to blow up into an unpredictable situation. The United Nations has been crippled for the past year because the United States used the payment of dues issue to tie up the voting ability of the General Assembly. When it appeared in the fall of 1965 that our nation could once again risk having votes cast in the General Assembly, our Ambassador to the United Nations stated that we would no longer insist that other nations pay their dues in order to vote. Although this is a matter of political engagement, it is also the way American Christians are related to the world's people.

Political Position

Furthermore, the stance taken by our government in the United Nations and elsewhere is determined by what political officeholders believe to be the best political position. The first and last law of a person in office is to stay there, and this means acting in the way the people who can deliver the votes want him to act. As long as the people in this nation want a cold war there will be one. However, there are enough people in the world who want an end now to the cold war to support the United States in a global war against hunger if a "Food for the Hungry" effort would promise also to help all people regardless of their religious, political or other connections.

The people of the United States are not ready yet to do this, in spite of the fact that Protestant, Catholic and Jewish positions adopted by high-level bodies would support such a global program. The General Board of the National Council of Churches is composed of representatives elected to it by the denominations, and although it states very clearly that it speaks only for itself it *does* speak from an established base of representation in twenty-nine denominations. On this subject it issued an important declaration. Here is enough of the statement to suggest its nature:

"We see a tremendous urgency in matters of hunger and food, in relation to our Christian faith, to our concern for human values, to prospects for the world's food demand and supply during the next several years and to basic economic and social development. Food is and will continue to be a key issue, and even more so if the U.S. continues a policy of relatively decreasing production in agriculture. Unless the U.S., with its outstanding capacities and world responsibilities, develops new concepts of larger production for programs related to world needs, the predicted widespread, acute famine in some areas of the world in the next few years will become more grim. Even more important is U.S. cooperation in helping other nations to develop their own food production and supplies. . . ." [4]

A move of this kind by the United States would be wise world politics, but it is unlikely that the American people are ready

---

[4] Quoted from the Resolution on World Hunger adopted by the General Board of the National Council of the Churches of Christ in the U.S.A. in June, 1965. Used by permission.

to support a program that would include sharing food with communist nations. The move would be wise because it would convince other nations that the United States can do more than defend the Dominican Republic or South Vietnam. Many individuals think that it would be unwise for American political leaders to support a "Food for the Hungry" program because there have been strong protests against every move to engage in substantial economic involvement with communist nations, which a move of this kind would mean.

A special group representing the National Council of Churches discussed the position taken by the General Board with several highly placed political leaders. These leaders were in deep sympathy with the position of the General Board, and it was noted in the discussions that Catholic and Jewish positions of almost identical nature had been adopted by equally high-level bodies. The main problem confronting the political leaders was the definite probability that it would be political suicide for any administration or candidate to urge such a line of action until there existed a prevailing public attitude favorable to it. No one present at the discussion thought that a global effort to end hunger on the earth had even a preliminary political chance of success. Here again is the problem of the attitudes of the prosperous keeping the poor in poverty, and attitudes are the stuff of which political support is made.

Attitudes are also the attributes of the human spirit with which the church deals in every way at its command. There is a widely prevailing notion that because an attitude is political it belongs outside the church's concern. It is not uncommon for individuals to protest with great vigor their pastor's interest in political decisions. Now and then a local congregation will take formal action condemning all forms of political involvement by denominational boards or officials. Below is a classic example of how some churches feel about Christian involvement in public issues. It is sufficiently altered to protect confidence but otherwise conveys the dismay of some Christians at the behavior of their brethren:

"Whereas it is the belief of this church board that it is not proper for the National Council of Churches or for The Methodist Church to participate in, or become involved in controversial, political and labor management problems be it therefore resolved:

"That the Board of the Xville Methodist Church does hereby express strong objection to the statement by Rev. Xname and to such participation in controversial and worldly matters by the National Council of Churches or by The Methodist Church."

The Nature of the Church

What do we do in such cases? Matters are made worse by engaging in conflict, with words hurled back and forth. There is desperate need for change in our understanding of the nature of the church in a politically structured world. The church in the United States is crippled when it comes to dealing with the political order because the attitudes of Christians are formed around the deep belief that religion is an internal and private affair. This view, as has been noted, has been developed with great care by Sidney Mead in *The Lively Experiment*.

The poor who crowd the globe are a long, long way from being interested in a Christianity devoted only to private faith as a source of internal comfort and a private sense of life's meaning. These may be necessary and no doubt treasured results of mature Christian religion, but when Jesus went out into the roads, the streets and the homes of people in cities, he spoke to them in their condition. He spoke to a man's sores and a cripple's limbs. He spoke to the rich man's sense of obligation and the calloused person's hardness of heart. Jesus was a troublemaker so far as satisfied people are concerned, but he was the Son of God for the outraged and the lively of conscience.

For those of us in prosperity, who have developed attitudes influencing United States behavior in response to global poverty, the issue is whether or not we understand our own predicament well enough to win converts to a line of action that will save us from extinction.

In Chapter I of this book I attempted to set forth a principle of history sound in Biblical and secular doctrine alike, stating that the future pours in upon us, and that this is God's action, destroying all that should not stand but nourishing all that should have growth. As a result, when that which should have growth has come to flower it also is flooded with the future coming in to test it, refine it and separate the worthy from the unworthy. Creation's way is an endless second-coming of God, a sustained end-of-the-world for some things and a sustained creation-of-the-world for others.

Standing in the middle of the stream of time is Jesus of Nazareth—Lord, Judge, Master and Messiah; but also Servant, Sufferer, Redeemer and Friend. What does he say to his churches in the United States?

He makes specific statements about food, birth control, education, farming, banking and political relationships. The conversion of our minds and hearts to the heart and mind of Christ on these issues is the price of our salvation, both physical and spiritual.

"The poor you will always have with you, and you can help them whenever you will," said Jesus when a woman lavished her adoration upon him and the atmosphere was perfumed with precious ointment. Obedience to these words of the Master would change the atmosphere of the world.

chapter X

WHAT THE METHODISTS ARE DOING

The Methodist movement is rooted in poverty. Part of the "methodical discipline" of the Wesley brothers and their Oxford associates was to visit prisoners. A majority of those in prison were there because of debts acquired in their dire poverty, and many prisoners were under sentence of death. The first societies (which later became Methodist Churches) operated on the basic assumption that none should suffer material deprivation. At the same time each person in need was helped to stand on his own economic feet. Wesley drew up a list of questions to be asked whenever the little societies gathered to sing hymns and study the Bible. They inquired: "Whether we may not lend small sums to those that are of any trade that they may procure themselves tools and materials to work with."

The contemporary war on poverty found The Methodist Church doing its traditional business. However, there has been a rising uneasiness in Methodist ranks that this business can no longer be carried on in traditional ways. In the present hour there is a lively reconsideration of Methodist procedures in ministering to the poor.

It is the purpose of this chapter to take a satellite's view of what the Methodists are doing around the globe in the war against poverty. In the following chapter we will examine some of the new and possibly more effective ways of pressing the war against man's ancient enemy of human deprivation.

In preparation for this chapter I sent a request to the executive staff of the Board of Missions. Each of the three Divisions (National, World, Woman's) replied to the request for brief thumbnail descriptions of actual programs in progress in the Methodist war on poverty.

The descriptions are in a folder slightly over two inches in thickness. I have read the entire lot, page after page, and I do not know what to do. Here is a story that would make every one of more than ten million Methodist hearts thankful for what is being done. Knowing this story would help each of these Methodists attend worship next Sunday with a new, vital sense of being connected with great purposes through the offering of money and self. The drab routines of much church involvement (necessary but often dull) would be brightened by the exciting knowledge that an official board meeting that dragged on until nearly 11:00 p.m. had reached out to touch some people in Bolivia or in a great city of the United States.

The story in the two-inch file cannot be told here. Maybe it will never be told. No other member of the staff of the Board of Missions of The Methodist Church knows all that is in that file. I am the only person who has read it and I am aware that I do not know everything involved in what has been described therein. After all is written that can be written, what are words?

But words are all we have, and with a keen sense of the hopelessness of my task, I will sketch something of what Methodists are doing. My hope at this point is that some individual in a local church will see a new opportunity for action and will speak of this opportunity to find out if God's Spirit is also speaking to others about a job that can be done in his church and community.

In Honolulu The Methodist Church has a community center. There was a time when some people thought it should be closed, and there was a very fine offer for the land. The buildings, quite old, are not long for this world. The workers in the center joined with the pastor and people of a nearby church to help school dropouts, of which the neighborhood had more than its quota. The program to help the dropouts led to a program for parents, which led to ministries in high-rise apartments and on playgrounds. The attitudes of the prosperous were influenced to accept as friends and associates some of the people whose poverty had threatened to cut them out of the larger community. To the workers in this community center it was all in the day's work, but they would not have been there in the first place had it not been for two things: their individual love and respect for the people they were giving their lives to serve; and the institutional church which paid their salaries and kept even that dilapidated piece of property in business. It should be noted that a new center will be built as inexpensively as possible because it is hoped that this area job will be completed in about twenty years.

Thousands of Methodists who know a lot about Goodwill Industries do not know that this great enterprise was born in 1902 as a Methodist ministry and is still related to The Methodist Church through the Board of Missions. In 1964 more than 50,000 handicapped people shared in its program of rehabilitation, job training and job placement. Goodwill Industries is the world's largest organization of rehabilitation centers with 131 plants now in operation in 11 countries. Plans are being considered to see if this type of enterprise can be adapted to rural situations. This year the Board of Missions is providing funds to set up another Goodwill center. About $35,000 is necessary to get a Goodwill unit on the way to self-support. In this work the prosperous show attitudes of trust, respect and full acceptance of those whose handicaps previously have made them outsiders, so far as employers and workers are concerned. Through Goodwill Industries people become insiders in the world of the prosperous and leave the world of poverty behind them. Probably they will not be rich in dollars but they will be among the self-supporting. What Christ incarnate means in this should be clear, but we suspect that many a local branch Goodwill manager would be reluctant to admit that he is giving self-respecting work to Christ—but what else could "you have done it unto Me" mean? Whether it is a "cup of cold water" or a job that gives self-respect, when it is done for human life, it is done to Christ.

Methodists and Education

How can we tell the story of the Methodists and education? Doors to a new and fruitful life swing open around the world for many an individual only because the Methodists believe in education. Most Methodists must know by now that the largest university for women in the world is a Methodist institution in Korea—Ewha University for Women. There are special and valid reasons for a woman's university there. Lodhipur Institute in India is another case in point. The globe is circled with educational institutions launched by Methodists but open to everyone.

In the United States Methodist schools are serving needs that would otherwise not be met. Let us name a few. Allen High School in Asheville, North Carolina, is a special school which sends its graduates out with full preparation for college work, although when they enter Allen High School they come as students with special needs. Among special elementary schools is Sager-Brown School where the students also have special needs that cannot be met by the regular school system. The Navajo Methodist Mission School has special doorways into the community of the wider world. The Robinson School in Puerto Rico; the Vashti School in Thomasville, Georgia; the Harwood School in Albuquerque, New Mexico, are names only to most readers, but to the people who enter their doors they are rooms for entering a better life.

It is easy to say that all citizens should be educated by the state or federal government. Tax funds should generally provide for the education of the citizenry. However, there are always special needs of people who for some valid reason cannot remain in the main stream and sometimes move ahead in it. They cannot manage at first without special help. Church involvement in education is justified in forms of ministry recognizing the personal worth of the individual who needs special aid in order to develop his personal resources to the point of self-dependence in earning a livelihood. Insofar as self-respect depends upon self-support in livelihood all Christians have an obligation to help their brothers achieve the knowledge and skills necessary to gain a livelihood. Christian influence in education is registered at this point of concern, whether the student is a Christian, Hindu, Moslem or atheist. If the student leaves the school a committed and disciplined Christian, this is all the better. If not, then Methodists have at least manifested a Christian attitude toward the non-Christian. This is a basic obligation. Education is a major weapon in the war against poverty, and Methodists should increase their use of it in new and special situations of opportunity.

Community Centers

Millions of Methodists do not know that they operate nearly 100 community centers through the National Division of the Board of Missions with funds largely supplied by the Woman's Division. In addition to these community centers, others are operated by annual conferences or city societies. To the last one these are engaged in the war on poverty. Let us consider a few examples.

The Bethlehem Center in Columbia, South Carolina, has a Job Opportunities for Youth project. Its purpose is to encourage school attendance while giving young people certain pre-employment experience after school hours. This project has expanded until more than fifteen community agencies plus individuals with special skills now meet each month at the center to plan strategy for the over-all community approach. This is a fairly normal example of the church engaged in what, for want of a better term, we call outreach. Perhaps it would be better to call it "inreach" because it is really the church in the act of opening up the hearts of the prosperous to welcome the poor.

A number of these community centers are linked to students in adjacent universities. Bethlehem Center in Nashville, Tennessee, is linked to Scarritt College, Fisk University and the University of Tennessee. Neighborhood House in Wilmington,

Delaware, is linked to the University of Delaware, and both Bethlehem Center and Wesley Center in Atlanta, Georgia, are linked to Emory University and the Atlanta School of Social Work.

During the summer of 1965 the headstart programs, designed to help children early in life, became familiar to the nation. By the fall of 1965 it was clear that the theory was sound: the time to begin education is no later than the fourth year. The community centers acted, and scores of cities had a headstart program because these centers qualified in terms of leadership, motivation and representation. This major front in the war on poverty may be the front most familiar to everyone. Methodists of Jackson, Mississippi, led a major program in headstart, integrated all the way, in the summer of 1965.

The community centers of The Methodist Church have been leaders in community organization and community development programs. Long before R. Sargent Shriver, Jr., gave national emphasis to the importance of having the poor assume responsibility for their own lives and environment our community centers were committed to this principle.

Bethlehem Center in Charlotte, North Carolina, took the leadership in forming a South Brook View Community Action Group, composed of residents and parents living in the area served by the center.

Other examples are the Rebecca Williams Community House in Warren, Ohio, the Newberry Center in Chicago, Illinois, the Northcott Neighborhood House in Milwaukee, Wisconsin, and the Church of All Nations in New York City. It is grossly unfair to name these and not others, but this suggests the spread.

One of the difficulties encountered by a community center when it moves into the work of community action and organization is the stout resistance that comes sometimes from members of Methodist churches located in the same city as the center. They look upon organization and action programs with real anxiety, because the evidence is clear that when people organize they want a few things changed. This upsets people who like things the way they are. It would be less than candid to pretend that all is peaceful in every city where Methodist community centers have become deeply committed to the needs of the people they are instituted to serve. There is serious tension between some prosperous Methodists and their brethren who live in the community of poverty. It is a tension rooted in housing conditions, lack of job opportunity, education issues and other sinful discrimination and exploitation.

Methodists who want things changed for those in poverty are, therefore, running up against Methodists who would like things to be different without being changed. Unfortunately, God will not let us have it so. Change we must if different we would be.

Two of our community centers are making outstanding contributions in the field of research for social work. Wesley Community Center in San Antonio, Texas, has a federal grant for research on the neighborhood approach to Mexican-American gangs. The Seattle Atlantic Street Center, Seattle, Washington, is in the third year of a study of fifty-four "hard core" boys from a neighboring high school, a study being made with funds from the National Institute of Mental Health.

Residences

Every year hundreds of young women leave small towns and rural sections to seek their way in cities. Many of them are trying to find their way out of threatened poverty or actual poverty. The Methodist Church has twenty-three residences for these job-seekers. While in these homes young women are provided with counseling on every possible level and are encouraged and assisted in advancing their education. Special concern is shown for girls who may suffer a physical handicap such as deafness, limited sight or limited mobility.

Fourteen homes for children and youth are operated by The Methodist Church on a national basis, and hundreds of similar homes are operated by annual conferences. There are no statistics on how many local Methodist churches are supporting children's homes of one kind or another. In these homes each child is offered an opening into the world of self-respect and social responsibility. One of the recently changed policies of these homes is a rise in age range which provides a much longer residence than in former years. The reasons for children being in the homes are different today. The motivation of the homes is the same: to serve as Christ served the needs of human life.

Hospitals

Methodist hospitals are a global story. Tuberculosis among native Alaskans was wiped out through the work of Maynard-McDougall Memorial Hospital in Nome and Wesleyan Hospital for Chronic Diseases in Seward. Clara Swain Hospital in Bareilley, India, is the oldest hospital in Asia for women.

Sickness is not always disabling and catastrophic. When it is, however, the individual is helpless. The person or family hit by catastrophic illness must often have doctors, nurses, hospital facilities and social welfare services during a long period of recovery. No one will ever know how many people have been kept out of poverty by Methodist hospitals.

What justification is there for church-supported hospitals? The main justification is in the upgrading of the tax-supported institution. The church hospital must be a better hospital, with better services and more lively ministry to the needs of the patient than the tax-supported or privately endowed hospital. In short, the Christian hospital has a right to church support only if it serves to set higher and higher standards for the community-based healing ministry. If Methodists do not have the best hospitals in the world they should have none at all. The Methodist Church is not a hospital system, an educational system or a system of community centers and welfare agencies. It is a Christian fellowship, and its involvement in these institutional enterprises is to set standards on an ever-ascending scale toward which non-church enterprises must climb. If Methodist-related institutions have not always been the best in the world, this does not invalidate the principle that their reason for being is based upon their excellence, and their excellence is measured by essential ministry to human life. If Christ is incarnate in the institutional ministry, let it thrive with our wholehearted support. If Christ is not incarnate, then let us find out why he is not.

The incarnation of Christ in the ministry to the physical needs of the poor has been a hospital witness of The Methodist Church for a long time. With the coming of new legislation such as Medicare, new avenues of service are being opened up, and we will deal with some of these in the next chapter. What Methodists have done and are now doing in the war on poverty in the field of health services should be appreciated as a substantial offering.

Appalachia

When the Congress declared the war on poverty, the word "Appalachia" got immediate circulation. Senator Robert Kennedy had just been elected a Senator from New York, and he probably surprised a number of people by insisting that the Catskill Mountains of New York are in the Appalachians. This is true, and the Senator got New York into the legislation.

The Methodist Church is in Appalachia and has been from the very first. Rev. Holmes Rolston of the High Point Presbyterian Churches near Bristol, Virginia, wonders whether in its present form religion in these mountains is an asset or a liability. A serious study, financed largely by a Ford Foundation grant, involved some prominent Methodists along with others. The study, published in 1962 as *The Southern Appalachia Region*, presents the findings of twenty-two research specialists who conclude rather generally that "militant, anti-scientific fundamentalism" is supported by fully one-third of the people, while the remainder have little or no access to any other expression of the Christian faith.

The Methodist Church in Appalachia is to a large extent a lay movement because it lacks situations able to attract and hold a trained clergy. This means that The Methodist Church in Appalachia has some of the virtues that go with strong lay participation and most of the weaknesses that go with the neglect of careful study and sustained reinterpretation of the meaning of the Bible and the nature of Christian history.

This came home with forceful impact when the National Council of Churches began to put its Anti-Poverty Task Force into action. This task force is supported generously by The Methodist Church to assist in making an interdenominational impact on the problem. The task force took as one of its first objectives the creation of a field staff, composed of trained personnel working with local church groups. By the time 36 workers were engaged in the program of this field staff, the region of Appalachia was still lacking in this service because no one in the 165,000 square miles of area could be found to take the responsibility.

In an effort to offset this, The Methodist Church is moving and has helped set up an Appalachian Planning Commission. This Commission will help coordinate projects already in existence, launch new ones and bring some together in new ways. For example, the Hinton Rural Life Center in North Carolina will be used as a training center, and all work in the Kentucky mountains will be restructured, with a new emphasis on local responsibility and local decision-making. The leadership of eight episcopal areas is involved in Methodist planning for Appalachia.

Appalachia is familiar country to The Methodist Church, but the size of the job has regularly been underestimated. Rev. Jack Weller, former director of the West Virginia Mountain Project operated by the Board of National Missions of the United Presbyterian Church in the U.S.A., puts it this way:

"Even the state government . . . has been unable to solve the problems we have been grappling with. The church has not been able to 'solve' any problem on the level of society in general

—whether economic, social, educational or medical. But we have been able to minister with some effectiveness to individuals entrapped by these problems." [1]

Appalachia is a mission field of a different kind. It is already "Christian" in one sense, but it is largely cut off from the main culture and will rapidly become even more isolated as the cybernetic revolution sweeps forward.

The Methodist Church certainly is not called upon to impose American urban and suburban culture upon Appalachia as part of its holy war on poverty. It may be that the full mission of The Methodist Church is to become involved in the full life of Appalachia in such a way that the people and cultures of Appalachia are accepted as precious to the whole stream of life in our time. Doing this will require of prosperous Methodists a change of mind, to accept different religious patterns and hymns and revivals along with attitudes toward work, play and love. Appalachia is not poverty-stricken in all things—not even in things economic—because there are rich areas here and there. Appalachia is a culture, and the contemporary, urban-minded Methodist Church is doing little to take advantage of what that culture has to offer the spirit of our times.

Every Methodist relationship to Appalachia should be led with the desire to let the spirit of Appalachia preach to us, sing to us, and lead us to see new qualities of life and death. To a limited extent this now characterizes projects in Jackson, Harlan, and Pike Counties in Kentucky, as well as others in the Holston Conference in Tennessee, but we have by no means gained the spiritual level essential for this mission with our brothers and sisters who, lacking money, have much else to give. Up to the present time The Methodist Church as a world body has paid very little attention to the needs of Appalachia. What has been done there has been with good intentions, representing desire to do good things. Today we know that this is not enough. The more that is required is the subject of the next chapter.

---

[1] Copyright 1965 Christian Century Foundation. Reprinted by permission from the July 28, 1965 issue of *The Christian Century*, p. 936.

The Methodist Church moved clumsily when the Economic Opportunity Act was passed by the Congress. The Roman Catholic Church provided an interesting contrast. Within a few days it issued its famous "blue book," a guide for the local parish, the diocese and the archdiocese. Through this guide bishops and parish priests knew the main features of the law as it related to new opportunities for the churches.

Protestant Slowness

Protestant churches as a whole were caught flat-footed in spite of the fact that they had been actively instrumental in getting the law passed. Even before Roman Catholics manifested interest in the widespread poverty of the nation Protestants had been gathering in solemn conclaves to ponder "Pockets of Poverty," and out of these consultations much of the drive and content for new legislation was derived.

But when the new law was voted, Protestants—including Methodists—were lacking in policy and methods of communication. In more brutal language, Protestants had nothing to say. Even if they had, it would have been impossible for them to say it because they were not organized to communicate a policy of community participation.

The question of possible violation of the principle of separation of church and state if a church served as a spending agent for federal funds came up immediately with the call for the Head Start program. For a while it appeared that Protestants would miss the boat.

What turned the trick was not Protestant vision and planning but community pressure. In one community after another it was found that the only agencies with rooms and qualified leaders were Protestant churches. Under community pressure Protestants entered the war on poverty through the Head Start program, and after they were engaged in action they began to formulate their policy. Reports indicate that Methodist involvement in this program was substantial. It will be a year or two before exact figures are available, but for better or for worse, a policy has come into existence.

Methodist structure is one reason why Methodism tends to neglect or fumble policy formulation on matters of this kind. Eight general boards serve as instruments of the General Conference on behalf of the denomination. Each of these is a policy-making body. The argument for a large number of policy-making bodies is that this insures a democratic structure, and this is a fairly convincing argument.

It could be argued also that the eight general boards have an obligation to hammer out their agreements on matters of basic policy at least to the extent that major legislation (almost always a long time in formation) does not catch the whole church unprepared.

In spite of the lack of policy on working with federal and state governments Protestants did fumble along with fair success, and Methodists probably did no better and no worse than the others.

But this is no time to delve into problems of policy and procedure. The two-inch pile of reports on the Methodist war on poverty is no longer in a neat pile on my desk. It is scattered and mixed, as my frustration mounts. How can the tale be told?

Missionaries in Action

Ten years ago a single woman missionary of The Methodist Church went to the most northern part of the island of Hokkaido in Japan. Winter is harsh there, and the people suffered horribly from lack of food. The missionary taught them home canning methods. They conserved the summer's product, and a Christian woman led them a few steps on their way out of poverty.

Okinawa is a name we know. Methodist missionaries are working with Church World Service to develop breeds of cattle and goats suitable for Okinawa's climate. Along with this they are working on the development of an inexpensive cattle dip that can be used by pioneer farmers. Thus does Christ walk his Galilean way.

Take a plane and fly north from Manila for an hour and a half and you will find some people with water and a special tractor. Until The Methodist Church put a man there, the valley was barren of crops and the people were starving. Now they have a well, the tractor turns the soil and pumps water, and the Cagayan Valley is green with growing rice.

Have you heard about the Congo lately? Your World Service is putting Methodist workers in the field there, and their ministry in Christ's form is in the shape of chickens, medical care, land development and instructions on how to use the good earth. Refugees from Angola in the Congo are being taught carpentry, tailoring, mechanics. Cybernation has not arrived as yet, but Methodists are helping people get ready for it when it does, and one does not start with a computer. The smart missionary is the one who knows where to begin, with steps not too big to be taken so that people walk on their own feet in today's mission.

Sweep around the globe to Uruguay and land in a section of Montevideo known as Valparaiso. You will see people scrounging in the garbage dump for anything they can find. The Methodists put up a building. The worker respects and loves the people, serving them in social case work, medical work, group counseling. Not all will escape from the dumps, but a few will. There is also a Sunday school, and there are services of worship.

In Buenos Aires, Argentina, some old streetcars were abandoned near the railroad yards. Central Church has converted them into a clinic, a school and a counseling office. Children come for storytelling periods.

North of Lima, Peru, is a dried-up river bed. In it is a place called Pedregal. In Pedregal a project similar to Goodwill Industries is under way, and Methodists have a program of preventive medicine. Plans are under way for a training school that might even be called a technical training institute.

Bolivia is a legend whose feature is poverty. For example, in the Mamore area the rich *patrones* exploit the poor the easy way, just forcing them to buy life's necessities at extortionist's prices. The few who farm get nothing for their crops. The Methodists have initiated a riverboat ministry taking spiritual help and medical assistance to hundreds of people living in these extremely isolated areas.

Methodists from the United States and Switzerland have worked with Bolivians to start a Credit Union. The poor in Bolivia pay as much as 120 per cent interest per year on crop loans. This Credit Union is designed to help them. You are there in your World Service dollar.

Let us go to Puerto Montt in Chile. Here there is a story of Methodist workers building chapels and spreading out to build others. Methodists are widening a circle of deep love and respect and sharing new forms of knowledge that open doors for those who have been helpless in their poverty.

Methodist Committee for Overseas Relief

For the past twenty-five years the Methodist Committee for Overseas Relief (MCOR) has been the conscience of The Methodist Church in moving out to meet the needs of the dispossessed. In this its service has extended beyond mere relief measures.

Emergency relief has been provided, of course. For instance, when an earthquake occurred in Chile, MCOR rushed to that country tents, blankets, clothing, food and medicines. Longer-range than emergency relief is the provision of farming tools in the Congo or vocational training in Korea, where orphaned children were for a time the primary responsibility of MCOR.

In the war against poverty the resettlement of families is a major necessity. More than 18,000 families have been helped by MCOR in finding a home in the United States, and for many of these the door from poverty into self-support was opened. Helping individuals start on a life of self-support has been done when MCOR aids in digging a well to get new land into production, as has been the case often in India. In a similar way, food-for-work projects in Jordan, Korea and Algeria have resulted in new roads, lands reclaimed from the sea and thousands of trees planted on barren hillsides.

The Methodist mission has always been a war against poverty, and the battle front reaches around the world. Something exalting speaks from two inches of reports.

Nevertheless, the attitudes of the prosperous keep the poor in poverty, and Methodists are highly placed among the prosperous of the world.

John Wesley feared that we would become sober, faithful, diligent, hardworking people who would gradually become well-to-do. For the most part his fears have come true, and now we are close to the bottom of the denominations in our stewardship.

The story of what Methodists are doing is wonderful—as far as it goes. It could be much more wonderful, with increasing satisfaction to each of us. As I look at the desk covered with reports of Methodist work around the world I do not know whether to rejoice—as I feel—or weep—as I feel I must—for Jerusalem.

chapter XI

WHAT THE METHODIST CHURCH SHOULD BE DOING IN THE WAR ON POVERTY

This chapter is a blueprint for action. It draws on a list of action objectives drawn up by various groups within the National Council of the Churches of Christ for consideration by the General Board of that body. On December 5, 1964, the General Board voted "to receive with appreciation the proposed Action Objectives for the Program of the Churches Toward the Elimination of Poverty, and commend these Objectives to units of the National Council of Churches, member communions, and state and local councils of churches for consideration as a resource, as they initiate and conduct anti-poverty programs."

If this chapter is a blueprint it has the values and defects of all blueprints. A blueprint is valuable because it gives shape to the job being done. It has the defect of thwarting creativity. Perhaps it will be possible for us to use this blueprint for action as a launching pad, rather than as a set of instructions. In that case we can drop the blueprint idea and, taking the action objectives as a starting point, orbit as far as we dare or as near as the situation requires.

In any case, we do well to begin by reminding ourselves that the church today exists on at least three levels: the local church, the denomination and the ecumenical relationship. The Methodist Church has a rather effective way of leaving the local church to its own strategies while holding all its local churches in a connectional system. The Methodist denominational level is really a service agency to the local congregation, but the local congregation makes the denomination possible. Methodist ecumenical commitment is greater than most people think. In spite of accusations here and there that Methodists do not believe in cooperation with other denominations, the facts show that a heavy portion of both finance and leadership in the ecumenical movement comes from The Methodist Church. This has been particularly true in the early efforts in the war on poverty. Methodists took heavy responsibility for providing both financial support and personnel to put into operation the Anti-Poverty Task Force as well as the Anti-Poverty Field Staff of the National Council of Churches. In addition, Methodists have launched a major interdenominational project in the form of Metropolitan Urban Service Training (MUST). Although committed to serving the whole community, this project is by nature aimed at the needs of the poor.

The Local Church

From the very first moments of the declared war on poverty there was a flood of inquiry from local Methodist churches asking how they could get into the war. This indicated a lively concern for the plight of the poor, but the inquiries were almost entirely concerned with some kind of relief project.

It is the burden of this book that relief projects will not do the job. The main task is to change the attitudes of the prosperous, for these attitudes keep the poor in poverty.

How does the local church go about this? The following specific suggestions will seem so simple to some that they will be dismissed at once. They lack heroism and offer no opportunity for doing noble deeds, either in the slums or in the so-called backwoods.

First, the local church should teach its members that people in poverty are not poor because they are lazy, shiftless, indecent and without motivation. This kind of education is not easy. It means that a prosperous (those with annual incomes above $4,000 per year) family must find some way to know a poor family without making the poor family (or individual) feel inferior, unequal, pitied or even a special concern. This kind of education is not acquired merely by reading books or by taking Sunday afternoon excursions into the ghettoes of poverty. Note, again, the cartoons in the front of this book!

One Methodist church had an imaginative pastor. He knew who were the poor people in the community. He took some of his more mature leaders into a training experience with role playing and other methods that can make humans of feeling out of cold, conventional straw men. He then assigned to each leader a poor family or individual, with these instructions: "We need these people to help us in our work of mission in education, worship, community action and world serving. It is up to you to get their help because we need what they can give to us and to others in the world."

This group of specially trained lay people succeeded in securing the help of several poor individuals who might have been considered worthless (at least to some degree) had the trainees not been helped to see the poor in a new way. One jobless man was put to work in the church helping sixth-graders prepare services of worship for their chapel hour. Much encouragement was necessary to keep him at it, because it was totally foreign to his previous experience. Encouragement to the effect that he was bringing a new quality into the youth service may have been the deciding factor. In any case, he became a changed person and changed others in the process. He got a job after six months, but that is not the real point. What happened was that some prosperous Christians changed their attitudes enough to realize that people in poverty have something to give.

This is an unusual case. Others who came into the fellowship of this specially trained group were able to give only their presence, and this on an irregular basis, but even in this there was a new openness that brought vitality into that local church. There was a genuinely new recognition of what poverty means. This particular church achieved a grasp of what some individuals lack, in a country where the current rate of general economic progress will find us in the 21st century before the average income of the poorest one-fifth of American families reaches $80.00 per week, at present prices.

Second, the local church can replace the attitude of condescending paternalism, prevailing in almost every community, with a genuine Christian understanding of the needs of the people who are a full human life. This means that the local church must find out what is going on in its local welfare agencies, relief offices and employment offices. One of the shocking scandals of our age is the brutality of the welfare and relief process in many cities and counties. Local churches cannot ignore their responsibility to observe, evaluate and patiently explore the processes in their local agencies. If these processes are good they should be encouraged. If they are brutal and paternalistic they should be helped to self-correction.

Third, the local church can make existing forms of worship and congregational life more meaningful and relevant, so that they will be a lively experience which the poor and the prosperous can share. If it really wants to, the local church can put an end to the charge that the church is upper-middle-class. This cannot be done by wishing. It must be done through radical overhaul of the services of worship and the kinds of congregational fellowship.

One Methodist church discovered that it did not have even one manual laborer in its official family, and some people thought that there were no such persons in the congregation. This told the church something about itself. Under careful pastoral leadership that church began to hold fellowship dinners, and for its speakers obtained union leaders, including shop stewards. It then formed panels to discuss what it means to be out of work. From that it went on to consider what it means to be on welfare. It would be claiming too much to say that the community was changed by this, but the church certainly was changed. It was touching an unfamiliar world, and attitudes were changed.

The worship experience in many a local Methodist church is out of this world—in the worst possible sense of the phrase—

which is not to say that worship often does not turn toward things eternal. That might be a welcome relief. The world addressed by the average service of worship in the average Methodist church is a world not now in existence. One strains to hear a word in hymn, anthem, prayer, Scripture or sermon that deals directly and powerfully with the present order. Of course we hear about the threat of nuclear warfare, automation and the coming leisure, but in terms so general as to arouse anxiety without opening the doors for decision-making and action.

Any local church today that brings worship and congregational fellowship to life around the specific needs of this world will find the power to meet those needs. It will be a Spirit-filled church, and probably it will be filled also with people.

Fourth, the local church can support the principle of involvement of low-income families in helping themselves. This is not new in theory but it would be new if many local churches took it seriously. One of the most controversial provisions of the Economic Opportunity Act has been its "maximum feasible" involvement of the poor in the war against poverty. In those places where the war is making the most progress this involvement is being supported. Local churches can win or lose the local war against poverty by their attitude toward this involvement. Sometimes this may mean clumsy handling of funds and program. It may mean more error in the trial-and-error methods of the war on poverty. A local church can help its community understand that the "maximum feasible" involvement of the poor in waging the war on poverty is justified in making mistakes that may be costly. After all, some space efforts at Cape Kennedy do not get off the pad!

The question of "maximum feasible" involvement of the poor in waging the war on poverty is hotly controversial in many parts of the nation. Why? Because it takes the war out of the hands of city hall and puts it where it belongs. In some cases this has meant that the poor have marched on city hall. No wonder there has been a political drive to remove the provision of "maximum feasible" involvement of the poor in leadership roles. The local church should be alive to this hot issue and ready to act, even if the mayor or a city council member is serving on the official board. A local church that swings public opinion to support "maximum feasible" involvement of the poor will be contributing a major social value to present and future generations. The local church can also invent ways of its own to involve the poor in their own war.

One rural community, with a number of low-income families, was helped greatly when the local church built a cooperative freeze-locker for saving vegetables and meat previously lost through spoilage. Many individuals could not afford to own and operate their own freezer, but they could manage the annual $12.00 rental of a locker. The economic value was important, but of more benefit probably was the sense of mutual accomplishment and the good feeling that the local church had been the main instrument of the project's realization.

Camping and recreational programs of local churches should be greatly increased to involve more and more low-income families of all ages. This is a door that many a local church has used in a limited way, but its use could be expanded easily if the congregation really sensed its power to bring a new vision into the lives of deprived people.

The formation all over the nation of "Senior Citizen" or "Golden Age" organizations in or by local churches should be understood in its full depth. One of the largest such organizations in the nation, with more than 5,000 members, found in its early stages of existence that it was difficult to get prosperous retired people to lend their talents to the project, which was heavily dominated by low-income people. Local churches were sponsoring the project, but energetic pastoral leadership combined with concerted lay effort was required to keep the prosperous in the project. At present the fellowship seems fixed with a mixed membership, representing a masterful example of pastoral and lay effort.

There are other activities in which a local congregation can engage in the war on poverty, but for Methodist congrega-

tions seeking a guide to local action these suggestions are
enough to start them on the right path. Once on the way
congregations will find new opportunities if they are ready
and willing.

The Methodist Denomination

We have said that the church exists on three levels. The
first is the local church, and we have mentioned some lines of
action and objectives for it. Now let us consider action objectives for the denomination, with full recognition that the
denomination cannot do a thing unless local churches support
what is being attempted.

The Methodist Church should increase its efforts to educate
its membership about the possibilities of economic growth.
Methodism should raise its voice and summon its membership to
support full development of the national economy through the
increase of industries and services. To those who believe that
this is not necessary, let it be said that the rate of economic
growth in the United States is being carefully managed to insure
that we will not have full employment—which is probably a
good thing—because too great a scarcity of labor almost guar-
antees inflation.

On the other hand, the prevention of inflation by the
preservation of a large unemployed work force raises ethical
problems no Christian can avoid.

At the present time the American economy is preserving its
energy through the encouragement of private spending and a
calculated control of the amount of money the government
spends out of the available total. There is no doubt that tax
reductions in 1964 and 1965 favored the prosperous and fueled
the economy. But what of the poor?

There is more ignorance than is good for us about how the
economic system functions, and the churches should take the
lead in bringing their membership up to date. The Methodist
Church can, and should, take the lead in giving its people a
grasp of contemporary economic theory and practice because,

in our time, theology and economics are tightly intertwined.

Related to this is the need for denominational recognition of the inequities in unemployment compensation. Only 40 per cent of American unemployed receive insurance. On the average, they receive about one-third of their regular wages, and this for not more than twenty-six weeks, except in a few states with extended coverage. No major improvements have been made in the federal plan since it was adopted thirty years ago.

In the Congress of 1965 a revision was proposed by the Administration. When it was presented, Secretary of Labor Wirtz said that the unemployed are ". . . people, men and women, who live in closets of depression in the mansions of prosperity." [2] It should be noted that this proposed change in legislation was not sent up to the Congress until August 9, 1965, and was the bottom item on the Administration agenda.

As a denomination, The Methodist Church has influential industrial, labor and community leaders who should be encouraged by their fellow church members to have this legislation raised to its proper importance. In view of the fact that many Methodists think of the unemployed on compensation insurance as "chiselers" this might take a little doing. But the attitudes of the prosperous keep the poor in poverty, and it is with the attitudes of the prosperous that the denomination must deal if we win the war on poverty.

The denominational program of The Methodist Church in its war on poverty will have to come to grips with the full meaning of discrimination in job placement, and will have to face also the lack of preparedness suffered by the average Negro applicant, through no fault of his own.

There is plenty of necessary work to be done in this country, but it is no small task to get the job and the worker together. Jobs that need to be done in Ohio cannot be done by persons living in West Virginia or Tennessee. Nor can a job requiring a strong physique be done by a man who has suffered malnutrition for thirty years without knowing it. Apple-picking cannot be done when an autumn day in Vermont may get no warmer than 35 degrees, and the apple-picker has just come from Puerto Rico or Louisiana where it seldom if ever gets that cold.

Job discrimination seldom takes place if a Negro applicant has a Ph.D. and is smarter than the rest of the Ph.D.'s, because it is "good style" to have a Negro around the place. Job discrimination has not been exposed for what it really is in most cases. Job discrimination is often no more than a reluctance to have someone around who somehow does not fit the established atmosphere. Even on a long assembly line there is a "style" the workers like, and if one does not have this peculiar and hard-to-define feature, life can be rough. If one has a contrary style, life is impossible, and the job is out of reach.

Nothing short of a denominational effort with special job-placement programs and job-preparation programs will meet Methodist responsibility to those in poverty because of job discrimination. The Delta Ministry in Mississippi, supported by the World Council of Churches and the National Council of Churches, has been hotly condemned, and all kinds of charges have been laid against it. One of the features of this program has been job-placement preparation. If the Delta Ministry had not taken an interest in voter registration it is conceivable that it would not have been under such heavy fire. However, if it stepped up its job-placement efforts it might be under even heavier fire. Major criticism came from those against its efforts to get jobs for Negroes in a firm that had promised to give jobs to Negroes, if the firm were given certain advantages at the time of its location of a new plant. The Methodist Church has given scanty support to the Delta Ministry. The attitudes of prosperous Methodists are offended by the radical involvement of the poor in Delta projects.

Methodist leaders in management, labor, finance, politics and education should be encouraged and inspired by denominational action to end the fear and suspicion now surrounding the effort to secure integration of workers on the job. Up to the present time efforts in this direction have been met by threats of withdrawal of funds for support of The Methodist Church. Whether or not to go forward in spite of these threats is a main policy question which cannot be left undecided. Obviously, it would be better if the attitudes of the whole denomination could be united around programs to end discrimination in employment, but the disclosure of the full meaning of this kind of discrimination, involving much more than mere job discrimination itself, will have to be made first. Such discrimination involves the whole life attitude of individuals toward individuals.

When we reach the point at which white and colored people can openly confess to one another that they have deep fears, anxieties and even rootless hatreds in their hearts for individuals of the other group, we may be able to discover what God is demanding of us in this whole situation. The Methodist Church is long overdue for a program of honest consultation involving white and colored people—north, south, east and west.

As a denomination, The Methodist Church should encourage the growth of community action enterprises through its local churches. To do this the denomination should establish a large number of training centers and support the effective centers established by other denominations. This is already being done to a certain extent. The Metropolitan Urban Service Training (MUST) project in New York City has been mentioned. This was set up by the National Division of the Board of Missions of The Methodist Church with a grant of $400,000. The Woman's Division later added $100,000. The function of this program is to train clergy and laity in urban ministry, and one feature of the program is training in community organization procedures.

In Chicago the Urban Training Center for Christian Mission, as well as the Ecumenical Institute, receives some support from The Methodist Church. These are training centers for both lay and clergy whose applications are cleared by the National Division.

The Glide Foundation in San Francisco and the pending development there of an Urban Training Center are additional cases in point. Meanwhile, there are Methodist Creative Experimental Projects all over the nation in urban, town and country settings.

This is not enough. There are 23,000 Methodist pastors, and for the most part these men and women are denied opportunities for re-training and re-motivation. They work long hours, meet heavy demands and often lack the experience necessary to help people engage in community organization. Large numbers of our pastors have not had the opportunity for significant outside stimulation for months or years. It is necessary for The Methodist Church to recognize its neglected ministers. Here and there are summer pastor's schools, and some pastors are able to attend, but it is common for a local congregation to insist that if its pastor is going to go to school he must do it on his vacation time, which is often limited to two weeks.

One of the most significant contributions that could be made by the General Conference and the Episcopacy would be a genuine revolution to achieve a change in the mind-set of the clergy and the local congregation, which limits the role of the pastor in such a way that he cannot be effective in community organization procedures. To the extent (which is, to my mind, very considerable) that our pastors are untrained in community organization procedures The Methodist Church is failing in its responsibility to win the war on poverty. This war will be won largely in terms of the ability of the community to organize its latent energies.

If The Methodist Church as a denomination does no more in the war on poverty than contribute to 23,000 communities (and more, for some ministers serve several communities) an effective leader in community organization, it might be the greatest single contribution the church could make to winning the fight against poverty.*

One final suggestion is made for the denomination. Housing is in many ways America's most complex social problem. The tradition of home ownership is still strong, but in great cities it is almost impossible to achieve. Those who buy with loans secured by federal or state provisions often have thirty years of debt. It may be assumed that many of these "purchasers" actually think of themselves as a new kind of renter or leasor. The question of providing housing for older people attracted the interest of the churches several years ago. Some of the best and most economical housing enterprises are church-owned and church-operated on a non-profit basis.

In September, 1965, new legislation was passed by the Congress to help provide housing for people in the lower-income brackets. In order to make sure that this program would not fall into the hands of speculators the law provides that housing built under its provisions must either be non-profit or "low dividend" in nature. "Low dividend" means that in the case of cooperative housing the rentals must be adequate to meet the costs of management and upkeep but not more than that.

In discussing this legislation Mrs. Flora Hacker of the Federal Housing Authority told the Anti-Poverty Task Force of the National Council of Churches that the success of this program would rest heavily upon the willingness of the churches to support its provisions through leadership in forming the necessary local or regional corporations to construct and manage housing.

Methodists could serve the public in a new way by forming a denominational task force that would direct the annual conferences in procedures leading to a fruitful participation in this program. To do so would not in any sense violate the principle of separation of church and state, because the housing constructed under the plan cannot be used for sectarian purposes in any way. It must be open to all. In this kind of action the churches would bring lay leadership into a social role of great importance.

Hardly a small town or city in the nation would not be the better for a project offering improved housing for the low-

---

* As this book was going to press the Methodist Board of Missions voted support of its National Division's proposal to extend MUST (Methodist United Service Training) on a national basis. In New York City MUST (Metropolitan Urban Service Training) is an interdenominational project launched by Methodist support.

income family. Nothing is quite as powerful in its influence over our lives as the place and neighborhood in which we live. When we meet a stranger we like to know what his name is, what his job is and where his home is. If his answer to our question about his place of residence reveals that we have some knowledge of what his neighborhood is like, we know quite a lot about the man. It may be superficial knowledge but it is the kind that counts to most of us.

In the first nine chapters of this book the thesis was developed that the attitudes of the prosperous keep the poor in poverty. This is particularly true in regard to the kind of place people live in, and it is sunlight-clear that millions of people living in places not fit for human life will never get out of those places without revolutionary changes in our housing procedures.

The Methodist Church is well equipped organizationally for a great contribution to American life on this score. It has jurisdictional identifications dealing with regional needs. It has annual conferences, which are corporations, already acquainted with state laws governing religious corporations. It has districts which generally operate with close association in matters of finance and government. The buying and selling of property and the building of churches and parsonages is an old story to Methodist district leadership.

There is already in existence in Methodism a national setup for a definite involvement in housing for low-income families. Two things are lacking, one of which must come on the denominational level, the other from the local churches. On the denominational level there should be a Department of Nonprofit Housing, located in the National Division of the Board of Missions. This would be a service department in much the same way as are the other units of the National Division.*

On the local church level there should be a demand for the advisory and counseling services of the Department of Nonprofit Housing. This might not be as likely to develop as one would think. Inertia in local churches, when it comes to matters

of this kind, is due partly to the hidden fear that real estate and
financial interests will be opposed to the local church. Even
district or annual conference involvement in such "worldly"
matters as building apartments for low-income families is likely
to draw fire. Also, the argument will be advanced, with some
piety, that: "We should not enter into financial contracts when
we do not know whether we will live to see the debt paid off."
The persons advancing this argument may be worshiping in a
church structure subject to a debt that will be paid only through
voluntary offerings of people over a period of many years. It is
strange how timid we are sometimes when it comes to doing
things that help other people have an easier and better chance
in life.

It is in the local church that the attitudes of the prosperous
will tend to keep the poor in their poverty-type housing. Not
because anyone is against the poor, but only because helping the
poor seems such a reckless undertaking—much more reckless
than building a beautiful church for the glory of God.

The Interdenominational Level

The Methodist Church exists locally, denominationally and on
the interdenominational level. The war on poverty presents some
situations in which denominations cannot act alone.

It is clear that Appalachia, for instance, requires a unified
approach, and this is being attempted through the formation
of an Appalachian Planning Commission composed of Roman
Catholic and Protestant leaders. The main difficulty with this
Commission, at the time this is being written, is its looseness.
It has no funds and no one to coordinate its efforts. Appropriate denominational officials are attempting to make available
the services of a highly qualified person to coordinate the energies of the Commission. If this is accomplished it will have to be
without fanfare. When interdenominational work is being done,
denominational contributions must be without denominational

---

* As this book was going to press the National Division of the Methodist Board of
Missions voted to establish a Housing Counseling Service.

boasting. Because word of denominational involvement does not always get around, local churches are usually denied the satisfaction of knowing that their World Service funds are being used to bring faith groups together into action. This applies to many interdenominational involvements of Methodists in the war on poverty.

Interdenominational involvement in the war on poverty should be increased. In a previous chapter it was noted that the poor crowd the globe and that global poverty will not yield to anything less than concerted effort. The choice of where efforts now to be applied will be most effective must be made in concert with Roman Catholics, Jews and other Protestants.

Efforts to supplant the current American image of policeman for the world with the image of the servant nation of the world probably would begin with an interdenominational appeal for relief of world hunger. In December, 1964, the National Council of Churches, through its General Board, *did* issue an appeal for a global program called Food for Hunger, and this was accompanied by similar appeals of Jewish and Roman Catholic bodies. The appeals were not followed up with strong nationwide efforts to inform the public mind and secure its consent. The war in Vietnam and the crisis in the Dominican Republic overshadowed everything else.

It is highly probable that Methodists as a whole do not favor a major extension of American aid to other countries. Throughout the nation there is a deep cynicism, feeding on deep resentment that others do not seem to appreciate what we have done for them. Is this not the same situation that prevails in a small community when the poor person who has been "helped" by welfare suddenly turns against the community and breaks into a liquor store or burns his own house to the ground?

The Peace Corps (an idea borrowed, we think, from Methodist J-3, K-3, US-2 and similar short-term service projects) is an indication of a better way to help, and the whole new concept of the meaning of the mission of the church to people of other lands is an asset we did not have ten years ago. We have learned much as a nation in this decade and we will learn more.

We simply cannot turn back from our world task. This task begins at home. It must. But it cannot end there. Not far from New York are nations whose children bear their first child at the age of twelve or thirteen and whose lives are condemned to an unbelievable poverty. These children will never be helped unless American Christians see to it that American people (Christians, Jews, atheists and agnostics) join in new ways of helping.

The great spiritual crisis of America is located in the attitudes that prevail in regard to the poor imprisoned in poverty. It is the task of the interdenominational church to give Methodism a clearer voice when it speaks and a suffering conscience when it does not act. Methodism on the interdenominational level is as real as Methodism on the local or denominational level, and on all three levels much is waiting for us to do. The issue is whether we are truly Christian as keepers of the poor or whether we keep the poor in their poverty by attitudes that we do not know we have.

theological postscript

The first chapter in this book is theological in nature. It takes the position that the future is not an empty room to be furnished according to our desires and powers. The future is thought of as an active power pouring in upon the present to baptize it with judgment and grace: judgment on the evil that is, and grace upon the good that may be. Today's good may become tomorrow's evil, in which case it will be judged for what it is. Slavery of men was better than slaughter of captured enemies, but in due time even slavery was found by the future to be an evil.

It is in something of this sense of the nature of the future that Harvey Cox in *The Secular City* speaks of the kingdom of God as the contemporary set of conditions to which man must respond with his "yes" or his "no." The kingdom of God is not something we build. It comes in upon us and demands our decision.

Certainly it is true that we did not plan events to produce the world around us. Science and technology have uprooted the old, familiar growths, and every pasture, glade and mountain is bringing forth new features of life.

Political structures and alliances refuse to stabilize, and while the population of the world outraces the food supply our skills at keeping people alive complicate our social predicament. Now and then is heard the insane suggestion that only a nuclear war will reduce the world population to a practical level, but no one seems to want to press for that solution—or for any other excepting what is vaguely called birth control. How to get the people of the world to practice birth control even when they know the method is another problem.

The collision of the great world religions is now occurring, and for the first time in its history Christianity is beginning to see that it cannot become the only world religion. It may be a good thing for the world that it cannot. Certainly, it is a good thing for Christianity that it cannot become the exclusive faith. This would be the end of Christianity so far as humility, servanthood and mission to others through suffering exist.

A shallow mind would conclude that things may have already gone to pot and the jig is up. Add to all the rest of human woe the urbanization of life with its contemporary brutality, and you do have a bleak picture.

In all this a theological mind would see the kingdom of God demanding man's response, in sacrificial devotion to the Lord of life whose claims upon his world are primary and final.

The poor in poverty are part of the kingdom of God. They live in our midst, while we who are prosperous would have them live to themselves. The poor are the people of God's love who have suffered the coming of old age, the accident of being born in a family of hardship or even the glory of being born non-white—a doubtful glory in a white man's town but a glory none the less.

Unless Christian people know that the kingdom of God is the future pouring in upon all of life, they will not respond in ways to escape judgment and receive grace. Judgment now rests upon our world and demands the ending of poverty. "Thy Kingdom come, thy will be done," that we may be the converted keepers of the poor.

We have no easy options in our response to the kingdom of God. What we do about our attitudes and our actions with regard to the poor in poverty is an issue of tremendous consequence. God does not let us live in a world without consequences. "The kingdom of God is among you" is not a word of comfort; it is a warning that our decision now will have consequences whether or not we want it that way.

The future is pouring in. The kingdom of God is come and is coming forever.

Whether we keep the poor in poverty or become valid keepers of the poor may be the question that decides the fate of the world.

FRIENDSHIP PRESS MATERIALS ON "AFFLUENCE AND POVERTY: DILEMMA FOR CHRISTIANS"

Adult:

Need Is Our Neighbor by Byron L. Johnson, paper, $1.75

Study-Action Manual on "Affluence and Poverty" by Mildred M. Hermann, paper, $1.25

Wealth and Want in One World, symposium edited by Muriel S. Webb, paper, $1.95

This Is the Puzzle of Poverty, pictorial and human interest book for adults and youth by Jeanette Struchen, paper, 85 cents

Next Move for the Migrants by William E. Scholes, paper, 85 cents

Dignity of Their Own, a report on the Migrant Citizenship Education Project by William H. Koch, Jr., paper, $1.95

Cooperation in Compassion: The Story of Church World Service by Harold E. Fey, paper, $1.95

Drama:

Two in a Trap by Allean Lemmon Hale, paper, 75 cents

Strangers Outside the Feast, a choral reading by Warren Mild, paper, 75 cents

Needs in Nutshells, four dramatic discussion starters by Braun, Eastman, Hilton and Irion, paper, 75 cents

"A" for Effort by Joyce Sloan, paper, 75 cents

Adult-Youth:

Are We Ready for Leisure? (Questions for Christians No. 5) by William P. H. Stevens, Jr., paper, 65 cents

What Future for Foreign Aid? (Questions for Christians No. 6) by I. W. Moomaw, paper, 65 cents

What's Mine: What's Yours? (Questions for Christians No. 7) by Jose Luis Velazco Medina, paper, 65 cents

Can Machines Replace Men? (Questions for Christians No. 8) by J. Edward Carothers, paper, 65 cents

All the above may be ordered from the Service Center, 7820 Reading Road, Cincinnati, Ohio, 45237.

Other materials for the theme, including materials for youth and children and audio-visual resources, also are available from the Service Center.

Chapter I.

Bornkamm, Günther. *Jesus of Nazareth.* New York: Harper & Brothers, 1960.

Boulding, Kenneth. *The Meaning of the Twentieth Century.* New York: Harper & Row Publishers, Inc., 1964.

Cox, Harvey. *The Secular City.* New York: The Macmillan Co., 1965.

Davies, W. D. *The Setting of the Sermon on the Mount.* New York: Cambridge University Press, 1964.

Heilbroner, Robert. *The Future As History.* New York: Harper & Brothers, 1959.

Toffler, Alvin. "Future As a Way of Life," *Horizon* (New York), Summer, 1965.

Chapter II.

Jeremias, Joachim. *The Parables of Jesus.* New York: Charles Scribner's Sons, rev. ed. tr. by S. H. Hooke, 1955.

Chapter III.

Horowitz, Julius. "This Is the Age of the Aged," *The New York Times Magazine* (New York), May 16, 1965.

McCanna, Henry A. "The Captive Rural Poor," *Information Service* (New York), September 11, 1965.

"Poverty, Affluence and Opportunity" (New York), a paper presented by Oscar Ornati, April 27, 1964.

Chapter IV.

Cameron, Richard M. *Methodism and Society in Historical Perspective.* ("The Methodist Church in Social Thought and Action," Vol. 1.) Nashville: Abingdon Press, 1961.

Cobban, Alfred. *In Search of Humanity.* New York: George Braziller, Inc., 1960.

Cox, Harvey. *The Secular City.* New York: The Macmillan Co., 1965.

Mead, Sidney. *The Lively Experiment.* New York: Harper & Row Publishers, Inc., 1963.

Niebuhr, Reinhold. *Moral Man and Immoral Society*. New York: Charles Scribner's Sons, 1932.

Re-Thinking Missions, A Layman's Inquiry After One Hundred Years. New York: Harper & Brothers, 1932.

Chapter V.

Berger, Peter L. *The Noise of Solemn Assemblies*. New York: Doubleday & Co., 1961.

Galbraith, Kenneth. *The Affluent Society*. Boston: Houghton Mifflin Co., 1958.

Leighton, Alexander H. "Poverty and Social Change," *Scientific American* (New York), May, 1965.

"Poverty, Affluence and Opportunity" (New York), a paper presented by Oscar Ornati, April 27, 1964.

Chapter VI.

Fingarette, Herbert. *The Self in Transformation*. New York: Basic Books, 1963.

Chapter VII.

Harris, T. George. "The Battle of the Bible," *Look* (New York), April 27, 1965.

Mead, Sidney. *The Lively Experiment*. New York: Harper & Row Publishers, Inc., 1963.

"The American Farmer in the World Economic Revolution." An address given at the National Farmers Union Convention by Gunnar Myrdal, Chicago, March 15, 1965.

Chapter VIII.

Smith, Adam. *Wealth of Nations*. Chicago: Henry Regnery Co., 1953.

Chapter IX.

de Castro, Josue. (Foreword by Lord Boyd-Orr). *Geography of Hunger*. Boston: Little, Brown and Co., 1952.

Myrdal, Gunnar. *An International Economy*. New York: Harper & Brothers, 1956.

"The American Farmer in the World Economic Revolution." An address given at the National Farmers Union Convention by Gunnar Myrdal, Chicago, March 15, 1965.

Pauling, Linus, et al. *On the Developed and the Developing*. California: Center for the Study of Democratic Institutions, The Fund for the Republic, Inc., 1965.

"Resolution on World Hunger." New York: National Council of the Churches of Christ in the U.S.A., June 3, 1965.

Vogt, William. *New York Times Magazine*. (q.v. in *Memo*), National Council of the Churches of Christ in the U.S.A., June 1, 1965.

Wolfle, Dael. "Save the World," *Science* (Washington, D.C.), August 20, 1965.

Chapter X.

Rolston, Holmes. "Appalachia: Mountains of Poverty," *Christianity Today* (Washington, D.C.), March 27, 1964.

The Southern Appalachian Region. Study sponsored by Ford Foundation, 1962.

Weller, Jack. "Ministering to Appalachia," *The Christian Century* (Chicago), July 28, 1965.

Chapter XI.

"Action Objectives For the Program of the Churches Toward the Elimination of Poverty in the U.S.A." New York, National Council of the Churches of Christ in the U.S.A., December 5, 1964.

"Resolution on World Hunger." New York: National Council of the Churches of Christ in the U.S.A., June 3, 1965.

Theological Postscript

Cox, Harvey. *The Secular City*. New York: The Macmillan Co., 1965.

Action Objectives for the Program of the Churches Toward the Elimination of Poverty 135
Affluent Society, The 64
Africa 86
aged 38, 39, 40, 41, 42, 45, 48, 146, 152
agnostic 150
Alaska 126
Algeria 134
Alinsky, Saul 32
Angola, refugees of 132
An International Economy 111 n.
Anti-Poverty Task Force 99, 128, 136, 146
Anti-Poverty Field Staff 128, 136
Appalachia 127 ff., 148
Appalachian Planning Commission 128, 148
Argentina 132
atheist 123, 150

Babylon 90
Baptists 87
Belgium 54
Berger, Peter L. 65, 78
Bible 85, 87, 118, 119, 128
Board of Christian Social Concerns 53
Board of Missions 119, 120, 121; National Division of 55, 100, 119, 123, 144, 145, 147 f.; Woman's Division of 100, 119, 123, 144; World Division of 119
Bolivia 120, 132
Bonhöffer, Dietrich 19
Bornkamm, Günther 19 n.
Boulding, Kenneth 17 n., 83
Boyd-Orr, Lord 105
Brazil 109
Buddhism 23, 71

California 20, 31, 100, 145
Cameron, Richard M. 53
Canada 110
Catholics 60, 80, 115, 116, 130, 148, 149
Chile 133
China 112
Christ (see Jesus Christ)
Christian ethics 35, 106, 111, 141; faith 96, 115, 127; individuals 96 ff.; way of life 80, 123
Christianity 15, 23, 24, 50 f., 71, 80, 117, 151
church, local 27, 98, 136 ff.; renewal of 84 f., 86 ff.; resources of 65 ff.; the captive 46, 52 f., 69, 73, 83 ff., 101, 102; the Christian 46, 52 f., 69, 73, 83 ff., 101, 102; the nature of 117 ff.
Church World Service 131, 132, 133, 149
cities 48, 55, 58, 60, 63, 66, 117, 120, 123, 124, 138, 139, 146, 147
Civilian Conservation Corps (CCC) 63
civilization 90 f., 113; post 17, 83, 89; pre 17
civil rights 78, 84, 92
clergy 65, 81, 87, 100, 101, 138, 140, 144, 145
Cobban, Alfred 51, 52
color, people of 38, 39, 42, 43, 45, 48, 67, 84, 144, 152
Colorado 30
communism 51, 54, 85, 86, 111, 116
community centers 55, 120 f., 123 ff.
community organization 32, 33, 34, 35, 55, 60, 124, 130, 137, 144, 145, 146
Congo, the 54, 132, 133
congregation, local 72, 78, 98 ff., 116, 135, 138, 145
Cornell Program in Social Psychiatry 59
Cox, Harvey 18 n., 50, 78, 151
Cuba 112
cybernetics 22, 50, 56, 67, 73, 87, 103, 109, 129, 132, 139
Czechoslavakia 112

Davies, W. D. 15, 16 n.
de Castro, Josue 105
Delaware 123 f.
Delta Ministry 143
Denmark, people of 93
denominationalism 87, 102, 115, 116, 130, 134, 135, 141, 142
Depression, the Great 63, 91
Dodd, C. H. 15
Dominican Republic 116, 149
drop-outs, school 42, 120

economic 24, 27, 31, 37, 42, 50, 51, 56, 58, 61, 62, 64, 66, 68, 69, 78, 91, 100, 108, 115, 119, 129, 137, 140, 141
Economic Opportunity Act 21, 31, 33, 46, 63, 65, 72, 73, 84, 130, 139
ecumenical 135 f.
Ecumenical Institute 145
education 19, 39, 44, 46, 48, 59, 61, 62, 68, 78, 80, 94, 118, 122 f., 125, 129, 137, 144
employment 36, 40, 68, 123, 125, 141, 142, 143 f.; part-time 39, 44, 45, 46, 48
England 95, 108
Episcopalians 87

farming 39, 44, 65, 78, 109, 118, 133, 134
Federal Housing Authority 146
Federal Reserve System 102
Fingarette, Herbert 71, 76
"food for the hungry" movement 112, 115, 116, 149
freedom 92
"Future as a Way of Life" 18 n.

Future As History, The 16 n.
"future pouring in" 15 ff., 89, 118, 151, 152

Galbraith, Kenneth 64 n.
General Conference 131, 145
Geography of Hunger, The 105
Georgia 122, 124
ghetto 55, 137
Gibbon 90
Glide Foundation 145
global hunger 111 ff., 149
God 15 ff., 25, 40, 50, 66, 70 ff., 106, 108, 117 ff., 125, 148; grace of 20, 151; judgment of 20, 151; kingdom of 15 ff., 29, 151, 152; will of 16 ff., 104
Goodwill Industries 121 f., 132
gospel, the 29, 80
government 19, 114, 128, 147, 173
guilt, feelings of 73 ff.

Hacker, Mrs. Flora 146
Harlem 84
Harris, Robert 16 n.
Hawaii 120
Heilbroner, Robert 16 n.
Hindu 123
Holy Spirit 101
hospitals 127 ff.
households headed by females 38, 39, 42, 43, 45, 48, 67
housing 93 f., 125, 146 ff.

India 72, 85 f., 86, 107, 108, 109, 122, 126, 134
Indonesia 112
industrialization 50, 70, 86, 109, 141
interdenominational 102, 128, 136, 148 ff.
Islam 23
Israel, people of 90

Japan 107, 108, 131
Jerusalem 74, 84, 134

Jesus Christ 15 ff., 29, 33, 65, 72 ff., 83, 96 ff., 117, 121, 126 ff.
Jesus of Nazareth 19 n.
Jews 80, 115, 116, 149, 150
Joachim, Jeremias 15, 29
Job Corps 97
Job Opportunities for Youth project 123
John XXIII, Pope 112
Jordan 134

Kennedy, Senator Robert 127
Kentucky 28, 128, 129
Keyserling, Leon H. 44
Korea 122, 133, 134

laity 65, 66, 100, 137, 140, 144 ff.
Latin America 108
League of Nations 52
legislation, anti-poverty 21, 35, 127, 130, 131, 146
Leighton, Alexander 59, 60 n., 62
Lively Experiment, The 53, 79, 117

McCanna, Henry A. 44 n.
Mead, Sidney 53, 79, 81, 117
Meaning of the Twentieth Century, The 17 n.
Medicare 88, 127
Melman, Seymour 72
Methodism and Society in Historical Perspective 53
Methodist Church, The 101, 117, 119 ff., 135 ff.
Methodist Committee for Overseas Relief (MCOR) 133 ff.
Methodist short-term service projects 150
Methodist Social Creed 53
Methodist Social Thought and Action (MESTA) series 53
Methodists 53, 87, 119 ff., 135 ff.
Metropolitan Urban Service Training (MUST) 100, 136, 144

Mexico 95; family of 30
migrant workers 45, 143
"Ministering to Appalachia" 129 n.
mission 50, 54, 67, 70 ff., 107, 114, 132, 134, 137, 150 ff.
missionaries 28, 55, 131, 132
missions 28, 49, 58, 70, 100, 123
Mississippi 124, 143
Moral Man and Immoral Society 52
Moslem 108, 122
Myrdal, Gunnar 85, 86 n., 111 n.

National Council of Churches Conference on Technology and Rapid Change 25
National Council of Churches of Christ in the U.S.A. 78, 102 f., 115 ff., 128, 135 ff., 143, 146, 149
National Institute of Mental Health 125
National Policy Committee on Pockets of Poverty 43
Negro 39, 84, 1.2, 143
Netherlands 108; people of 93
New Testament 15, 50, 98
New York 34, 41, 47 f., 84, 95, 99 ff., 113, 124, 127, 144, 150
New York Times 82
New Mexico 122
Nobel Prize winners 105, 113
Noise of Solemn Assemblies, The 65, 78
North Carolina 122, 124
nuclear dangers 23, 82, 139

Office of Economic Opportunity (OEO) 21, 26, 36, 46, 63 ff.
Ohio 124, 142
Okinawa 131
Old Testament 50, 90

On the Developed and the Developing 113 n.
Operation Head Start programs 13, 124, 130
Ornati, Oscar 32, 38, 39, 64

Pacem in Terris (Peace on Earth) 112
Pakistan 108, 109
Papal Encyclical 112, 113
Parables of Jesus, The 29
Pauling, Linus 113 n.
Peace Corps 150
Pennsylvania 84, 100
Peru 132
"pockets of poverty" 21, 43, 130
political 21 ff., 29, 51 ff., 58, 63, 68, 79, 86, 114 ff., 118, 139 f., 144, 151
Poland 112
"Poverty and Social Change" 60 n.
poverty-linked characteristics 38 ff., 48, 60, 64, 67
poverty-population law 107 ff.
prosperous, conversion of 33 ff., 68 ff.
psychiatry 70 ff.
Puerto Rico 122, 143

Rauschenbusch 50
relief programs (see welfare)
religion 15, 23, 50, 52 f., 68, 79 f., 87, 93, 117, 129, 147, 151
residences 125 ff.
Re-Thinking Missions, A Layman's Inquiry After One Hundred Years 49 n., 50
Road, the 59 ff.
Rogers, Carl 81
Rolston, Holmes 127
Rumania 112
rural 32, 43 ff., 49, 55, 63, 140, 145
Russia 110

"Save the World" 106 n.

Scandinavia 108
Secular City, The 18 n., 50, 78, 151
Self In Transformation, The 71
"Senior Citizen" organizations 140
Setting of the Sermon on the Mount, The 29
Shriver, R. Sargent 26, 124
Smith, Adam 91 .
Social Security 41; Administration 38
socialistic 85
Southeast Asia 86, 114
South Carolina 124
South Vietnam 116
stewardship 134
suburban 65, 129
Suburban Captivity of the Churches, The 78
Switzerland 133

technology 25, 42, 45, 86, 87, 151
Tennessee 123, 129, 143
Texas 125
"The American Farmer in the World Economic Revolution" 86 n.
"The Captive Rural Poor" 44 n.
The Southern Appalachian Region 127
Thoreau 68
Toffler, Alvin 18 n.
Toynbee, Arnold 90

United Nations 114; Food and Agriculture Organization of 105; General Assembly of 114
United States 13, 14, 20, 40, 54, 55, 62, 69, 85, 86, 87, 91, 92, 95, 96, 100, 101, 103, 110, 112, 114, 115, 117, 118, 120, 122, 123; Bureau of the Census 42; Chamber of Commerce 26; Congress of 21, 64, 65, 72, 96, 100, 112, 127, 130, 142, 146; Department of

Agriculture 43; Senate Foreign Relations Committee of 105
university for women, largest 122
urban 32, 43 f., 96, 100, 129, 145, 152
Urban Training Center for Christian Mission 145

Vatican, the 24
Vermont 143
Vietnam 114, 149
Virginia 127

Walden Pond 78
war against poverty 19, 20, 21 ff., 27, 37, 57 ff., 63 ff., 74, 123, 133
war on poverty 35, 47 ff., 58, 119, 127, 129, 130, 131, 135 ff., 142, 145, 148
Ware, Thomas 105
Watts, Los Angeles 20, 31, 100
Washington 125
Washington, D. C. 100
Wealth of Nations 91
welfare 29, 36, 41, 43, 47 ff., 59, 73, 88, 126, 133, 138
Weller, Jack 128, 129 n.
Wesley, Charles 119
Wesley, John 52 f., 119, 134
West Germany 108
West Virginia Mountain Project 128
Wilder, Amos 18
Winter, Gibson 78
Wisconsin 124
Wolfle, Dael 106 n.
Work Progress Administration (WPA) 63
World Council of Churches 24, 143
world population 105 ff., 151
worship 82, 85, 98 f., 120, 132, 137, 138 f., 148

Yugoslavia 112; people of 93

Joint Commission on Education and Cultivation
Board of Missions of The Methodist Church
Service Center, 7820 Reading Road, Cincinnati, Ohio 45237
Price, $1.00